TREASURES

within the Box

TREASURES

within the Box

WITCHCRAFT, RAPE, AND BETRAYAL
THE GEMS SAVED, A WARRIOR MADE

Paula R. Box

2 Timothy 1:7

Paula R. Box

COPYRIGHT PAGE

Where is the Lord God of Elijah?
2 Kings 2:14

Special Note In this book, the author has chosen to capitalize all pronouns referring to the Godhead—Father, Son, and Holy Spirit—as a sign of honor and reverence. Conversely, the name of satan and related titles have not been capitalized. We choose not to acknowledge him, even to the point of violating standard grammatical rules.

Published by: Firepower Scrolls
Facebook: Firepower Revivals
Email: firepowerrevivals@gmail.com
ISBN: 979-8-218-91813-2
First Edition
Printed in the United States of America

"I will give you the treasures of darkness and hidden riches of secret places that you may know that I, the Lord, who call you by your name, am the God of Israel." — Isaiah 45:3 (NKJV)

FOR I KNOW THE THOUGHTS THAT I THINK TOWARD YOU, SAITH THE LORD, THOUGHTS OF PEACE, AND NOT OF EVIL, TO GIVE YOU AN EXPECTED END.

JEREMIAH 29:11

DISCLAIMER

This book is a collection of personal testimonies based on my true spiritual journey. It reflects my personal recollections of experiences over time. While the events and emotions are real, certain measures have been taken to protect the privacy and safety of others. In the spirit of discretion, various details and identifying characteristics have been modified. These adjustments serve to safeguard the privacy of those involved while maintaining the core truth and spiritual essence of the encounters.

Readers should be advised that certain accounts contain raw and graphic descriptions of life experiences that may be intense for some audiences. This narrative represents my personal perspective and is not intended as medical or psychological advice. If you have any health-related questions, please consult with a licensed professional and seek God with the doctors for your own path of directions. This work is not intended to disparage any individual, but rather to reveal the treasures of victory I found through faith.

Book Production Credits The author gratefully acknowledges the professional services and creative contributors who assisted in the preparation, design, and technical production of this manuscript.

BUT WE HAVE THIS TREASURE IN EARTHEN VESSELS, THAT THE EXCELLENCY OF THE POWER MAY BE OF GOD, AND NOT OF US.

2 CORINTHIANS 4:7

DEDICATION

To my mother, whose love was the first treasure my soul ever encountered. Though you have entered your eternal rest with the Father, the seeds of your faith and the weight of your legacy continues to flourish through every branch of the family tree that you so lovingly and divinely helped shape.

To my loving and powerful daughter, Cammy Ferrell. May you always walk in your God-given birthright, picking up the mantle and smiting the rocks before you. May you always carry the legacy, remaining in confidence that your heavenly Father goes before you. May you always be mindful of the souls that are crying out for a drink of that holy water you have been so blessed by God to carry. And I know you will raise Roman to do the same, since God has already shown me this in a dream before he has even left your womb. Carry on, mighty woman of valor, and make mama proud! All Heaven is backing you!

And finally, to the ones who feel shattered, forgotten, and tossed into the hidden shadows of the deep. To the survivors of the silent wars, whose scars are the evidence of battles fought in the secret places that they were too afraid to talk about: this book is for you. May these enclosed words be a tool used as you navigate your way out of the darkness. I declare that the chains of your past are breaking, and you shall find the untapped treasures within your own personal treasure box. It is time to reclaim your priceless diamonds and pearls that have been buried within you all along—for the King is calling you forth by name into His divine presence.

TABLE OF CONTENTS

ACKNOWLEDGMENTS

First and foremost, I acknowledge the Father, Son, and Holy Ghost. Without the King of Glory, I am nothing; yet through Christ, I can do all things. He is the lover of my soul, my All-Sufficient One, and the Author and Finisher of my faith.

In that same spirit, I want to express my deepest gratitude to those who have been there from my cradle, the past twelve years, and even up to the present time. To everyone who has prayed, laughed, cried, and walked with me through every shifting season: thank you. Within this circle, I especially honor the joy-bringers who lightened my load and the watchmen who stepped onto the front lines of the battlefields with me to engage the powers of hell in the midnight hours while the storms raged. Thank you for having my six, for sharpening me, and for believing in God's ministry He has entrusted to me.

I recognize that every soul who has crossed into my life was a gift from the Almighty. I understand now that some were only meant for a season, as the Word says: "They went out from us, but they were not of us..." Regardless, I am thankful for the lessons they taught me and the God-orchestrated departures that allowed the sovereign hand of the Father to remove them from my circle, because we all know that God will not allow everyone access to our next levels. I stand anchored, knowing the Father is divinely navigating my course—preserving a steadfast remnant while gently releasing what has already served His purpose. Regardless of the length of time you stood by me or the role you played, I am thankful for every unique thread you wove into the tapestry of my life.

Thank you.

With a heart of thanks, I acknowledge those who have been the hands and feet of Christ in my life: The late Prophetess Maxine Box, my precious and loving mother; Charles Box, my incredible sweet daddy—Dad, I don't know where I would be without you; Prophetess Cammy Alexis Ferrell-Box, my loving, strong, courageous, and wise daughter; Roman Paul, my grandson, whom God showed me in a dream while you were yet in your mother's womb—you shall surely pick up the spiritual mantle for the next generation, and I cannot wait to meet you; Chuck Box, my knowledgeable, awesome and called by God brother; Julie and Billy Headley, my steadfast, life-saving sister, ordained for the grace-filled journey that awaits you in the seer seat; Donna Box, my niece and prophetess who is forging forward in her calling; David and Ashlie Box, my nephew and the next battle-axe of deliverance for the Lord in the family lineage; Brittany Headley, my brilliantly called by God and beautiful niece; and all my great nieces and nephews who are currently being trained under the adoration of the Lord Jesus Christ by their parents: Makayla Patterson, Aaliyah Patterson, Derek Patterson, Noah Box, and Asher Box. The late Mable Quick, my Grandma, Matriarch, and Pastor of the Quick family. Aunt Myrtle and Dale Martin, my fireball, Holy Ghost-filled auntie whom I adore, who is still faithfully pastoring today. The entire Box family; The entire Quick family; Mandy Barker, Chosen Kin and prophetic warrior; the late Pudding Tane McKenzie, precious and funny; Elaine Perez, Anointed devil-stomping Intercessor; Kathy Osborn; Powerful man of God Prophet Pat Galvan, Anointed Prophet; the late Reverend Samuel Martin; the late Pastors John and Dodie Osteen; the late Apostle Gene Doyle; Apostle Lorine Doyle, my precious mother in the Lord; the late Prophet Billy Griffin; the late Prophet Alfred Covey; Ronda Covey; Terrie Dunn, Pastor Betty Miller, the late Pastor Ted Woods; Pastors Joe and Barbara Washburn, Pastor Jo Schwake, Pastors Brooke and Beaux Jones, Tino Aguillon, Louis Findley and the gang; Buddy Galvan, Rachel Munoz, Prophet Al and Yanti Cavozos, Minister Jessie Caballero, Pastor Lolly Caballero, Prophet Tom and Debra Boozer, Evangelist Chad Garrett, Apostle Robert Clancy, Faye Bishop, Juanita Snow, Cat and Dustin Doyle, Cat Trulove, Prophetess Barbara Gaines, Minister Deborah Elum, Pastors Sean and Aimee Pinder, Prophetess LaCricia Hlavinka, Pastor Gary and Neiosha Young, Pastor Kimberly Sutton, Billy Starks, Arletta Hightower, Brandie Fournerat, Katherine Ferguson, the late Sis. Pat Alcala, The Doyle family, The Edwards family, The Henderson family, The Lott Family, Pastors John and Patti Smith, Pastors Veronica and Gustavo Batres, Pastors Pricilla and Julio Rico, Pastors Leticia and Jose Lopez, Apostle Maria and Eliseo Alarcon, Apostle Florentino and Maria Oliva, Evangelist Maddix and Ebony Jones, Prophet Wade, Pastor Marvin, Shelia and the late Reggie Warren; Rick Collins, Shawn Hernandez, Johnny Price, John Alberth, and all my Honduras and Colombia families.

WHERE IS THE LORD GOD OF ELIJAH?

2 KINGS 2:14

INTRODUCTION

I have endured the kind of torture and soul-crushing pain that was designed to silence me forever. Yet, I stand before you today, deeply grateful to be in my right mind—not locked up in a mental hospital and not in a grave pushing up daisies. I have moved from merely surviving to truly thriving, and I have finally found my desire to live again. My experiences are not shared for your pity; they serve as a living witness that no matter what the devil puts you through, God is a faithful Father. I found that with His mighty hand of deliverance, He knows exactly how to keep His children sheltered and safe. God is all-powerful. He is able to snatch us from the pits of a devil's hell, even when we ignorantly placed our own bed there. He desires to deliver us more than we can possibly imagine; we simply need to give Him the chance. Throughout these chapters, you will witness how I eventually turned to the Master of the Sea of Galilee amidst my own storms and found there is no distance too great for Him to reach us. I discovered that in His presence, there is no wound He cannot heal and no storm He cannot command to be still.

I must admit, forgiveness has been my greatest lesson during the many years of my journey that you will read about in this book. I have learned to forgive and stand by putting my hand in the nail-scarred hands of

Jesus. With His amazing grace, He truly gives beauty for ashes. Our God is a Restorer. He is faithful to give double for our troubles and to restore every year the cankerworm has destroyed. With Christ Jesus, a beautiful ending is possible—one filled with love, peace, hope, and joy unspeakable and full of glory.

This book reveals my journey through the fires sent by hell itself and how I emerged on the other side without the stench of smoke. I have written about the good, the bad, and the extremely ugly. However, I stand firm knowing today that I am not a victim but a victor, and I am truly a new creation in Christ Jesus: 2 Corinthians 5:17. I no longer live in the painful chapters of yesterday but in the realms of Glory in the here and now. I now desire for everyone I meet to experience the same. I feel this is more than just a book of testimonies, it is a manual of survival for every precious jewel currently being refined in the furnace of affliction. Just as restoration was mine for the taking, I wrote this to encourage you that the very same victory is waiting for you. As you turn these pages, I pray you find the strength to surrender all to God and step into the waters of total freedom that are flowing just for you and receive more than you could have ever imagined from your faithful Creator.

PRAYER

Heavenly Father, I lift up the one holding this book right now. I thank God for their life and for the divine appointment that has brought them to this book. I cover them now with the precious Blood of Jesus Christ. I decree that as they journey through these truths, a hedge of protection is set about their mind, their heart, and their home. I rebuke every demonic spirit that would try to hinder or distract them from finishing these pages, for I decree that every word written here is a seed of total freedom.

Holy Spirit, grant them the strength to be open and honest, with the grace to be vulnerable before the throne, knowing that help and protection are found at the feet of Jesus. I pray they will search their hearts and release every lingering wound into the hands of the Master Physician today. I thank You, Lord, that even as they read this book, your powerful and skillful hand is reaching down to remove every hidden root, and not one stone will be left unturned.

As these layers are removed, I pray they will see themselves through your eyes, Lord. Let them realize they no longer have to remain a victim in life, but that they are truly victors rising out of the fiery furnace. Lord, I thank you for the rare and resilient diamond they are, safely held and cherished in your hands. I pray that as they emerge from this book, the light of your glory would hit every facet of their life, polishing every area where it is needed.

I thank you for helping them to let go of the ashes so they can pick up the beauty that awaits them. I thank You that once the Master has completed His divine process, they will shine so brightly that they, too, will be able to open their own treasure box for a hurting world to see and partake of the heavenly gems found within.

I seal this prayer in the matchless and mighty name of Jesus Christ. Amen.

CHAPTER ONE

ROYAL BLOOD

I was a chunky little monkey with curly blonde hair and gray eyes when I was born in nineteen seventy-four, in a small city called Conroe in the big Lone Star State of Texas—just forty miles north of Houston. My parents wanted to name me after my grandfather on my dad's side of the family; his name was Paul, since they were told they would be having a baby boy.

However, the ultrasound machine did not reveal the correct information. When I arrived as a surprise and they realized they had a girl on their hands instead of a boy, they simply decided to add an 'a' to the end of my name. By simply adding an 'a' to the end, the feminine version was born—and voila!

There you have me, Paula: very much a thorn in the flesh and a devilish hot mess to many as I was growing up. However, later when I found the Lord, he began to show me who I was in him and how I 2had actually been called to the nations. This is when things majorly shifted, and we will discuss the process of that shift in this book of testimonies. I can truly attest to the scripture being true in Jeremiah 1:5: "Before I formed you in the womb I knew you; before you were born I sanctified you; and I ordained you a prophet to the nations."

I truly believe this calling on my life must have been a generational inheritance, forged in the fires of a praying family. Even though I was not personally brought up in church nor taught about the Lord. My mother, on the other hand, was raised by the sounds of "Brush Harbor" meetings echoing in her front yard and seeing the supernatural powers of God in full operation as a young child. This is where my grandmother and her sister would stand to preach the Word with the convicting power of God and demonstrations of the Spirit.

Eventually, my grandfather and great-uncle built a church specifically for them to minister in—a building that still stands today in Missouri. We seem to have more women ministers than male ministers for some reason, though in our family lineage. Also, oddly enough, I have always felt there has been a link between my family and Kathryn Kuhlman's ministry. I am convinced Kathryn Kuhlman was the catalyst for the ministry in our family bloodline.

My grandmother and Kathryn were practically neighbors, living in such close proximity that it is hard to imagine their paths did not cross. Especially, as pioneering women, who were being used to set Missouri ablaze, one meeting at a time, during that same era. Perhaps my grandmother sat in one of her meetings, or maybe she was simply moved by the wake of the revival Kathryn was being used to birth all throughout the land.

Looking back, I see that a seed of holy boldness was planted back then, giving the women of my family the strength to stand and not be silent during a time when the world tried so desperately hard to hush their voices—even as they try to silence women ministers to this very day. Because my grandmother and her sister, no doubt, preached with boldness and authority, without holding back. They made sure the sounds of the Gospel continued to ring out as they labored to help set the captives free.

Funny enough, to this day, I have people whom I do not even know, and who have never met any of my family, randomly come up to me in meetings to tell me they feel I carry that same Kathryn Kuhlman style of anointing on my own life. My family members will tell me that I sound just like my grandmother—preaching loud and preaching fast, like a train that will not be stopped!

I must always laugh, though, and tell them, "Now, you know—Aunt Myrtle takes the cake when it comes to fiery preaching!" Aunt Myrtle remains a living emblem of this unquenchable fire, as she continues to faithfully follow in her mother's footsteps, plowing the spiritual soil of Missouri even into her eighties. She reminds me of a Holy Ghost Energizer Bunny when she steps behind the pulpit of her church, releasing that holy war cry before the heavenliest. Thanks be unto God, though and his

Holy Ghost and fire, that is keeping us all alive—because that alone is a testimony in itself. It is all about our good Lord above and his sustaining grace to give us the ability to do what we do.

Many who are called by God, much like certain members of my family and myself, will be able to relate to this particular chapter. This chapter will reveal how the enemy tries to destroy those whom God has created at an early age, all because of the hidden treasures within their God-given spiritual treasure boxes.

When we are born, the enemy waits for no one; he begins his assault as quickly as possible to start destroying our divine destiny from God. Why might you ask? It is simple: he is afraid of your success and mine through Christ Jesus our Lord. He desires to strip us of our calling because he knows we will help populate the kingdom of Heaven, pulling souls out of the clutches of a burning hell and sparing them from an eternity filled with unquenchable flames. In the pages to follow, I will expose the enemy's evil plans through the lens of my own life and the stories of others. These are more than just stories; they are testimonies of a God who specializes in turning our deepest tragedies into magnificent triumphs.

A great biblical example of the devil trying to assassinate a child before he could even dirty his first diaper—let alone fulfill God's assignment on his life—would be none other than the Red Sea splitter himself: good old Captain Moses. You see, at the time of Moses' birth, the current Pharaoh had decreed the death of all newborn male babies. Moses, having just been born, fell directly under that death decree.

We can read how this transpired in Exodus 1:8–10: "Now there arose a new king over Egypt, who did not know Joseph. And he said to his people, 'Look, the people of the children of Israel are more and mightier than we; come, let us deal

shrewdly with them, lest they multiply, and it happen, in the event of war, that they also join our enemies and fight against us, and so go up out of the land.'" And in Exodus 1:16, the command became even more lethal: "...and he said, 'When you do the duties of a midwife for the Hebrew women, and see them on the birth stools, if it is a son, then you shall kill him; but if it is a daughter, then she shall live.'"

The Pharaoh here was being used by satan to destroy Moses. In this account, we see the Pharaoh's fears were of the Israelites prospering in the land and overtaking the Egyptian people. Just as he fears now—the ministers of God taking over his earthly camps. Thus, the decree from the king went out to kill all the male babies. We see a murdering spirit arise when someone called of God is about to be born—someone whom God desires to use.

However, later in this story, as most of you already know, God delivered the soon-to-come deliverer. God worked it out in this story so that Moses was spared from death, and in the end, his own mother was able to nurse him. Not only was his mother able to nurse her child who should have been dead, but Pharaoh's daughter paid her to do it! How many women get paid to take care of their newborn babies? The Bible does mention that when the enemy steals from us, we are entitled to a sevenfold restoration in Proverbs 6:31.

The devil's plans had backfired once again! God had already ordained Moses' assignment before Moses was even born. God ordained Moses' footsteps before the very foundations of this world had been laid. Just as God has ordained mine and yours as well. Moses' assignment was to eventually deliver God's people from bondage, many years in the future, out of the land of Egypt. Moses' life was spared by God because he still had a mission to fulfill! Just as you and I have both been spared—still alive and breathing—so we too can carry out the divine mandate given to us by Heaven itself.

I know I used Moses as an illustration here, but the Bible is filled with so many more brave soldiers besides Moses whom the enemy tried to kill. Of course, I am sure we can all agree that the story of The King of Glory, Jesus Christ, himself is our favorite all-time story ever. From his very first breath, the enemy sought him fiercely, strategically hunting him from birth until his appointed hour. It was a chase from the cradle to the crown.

Yet, on the cross of Calvary, he chose to lay his life down and give up the ghost on our behalf; swallowing up death and snatching away its sting forever, as he stormed the gates of hell and took the keys. Through that divine exchange, his death became our eternal life—granting us the keys to our very own mansion. For all those who accept him as Lord, this is where the gates are made of pearl, the streets are paved with pure gold, and the walls are built of jasper; the place we call Heaven. If the very dirt of his home is made of pure gold, just imagine the priceless investment and eternal value he has hidden within the spiritual box of your life.

This is the reason most of us have been under such intense warfare; the enemy has always been able to sense the weight of God's glory, even while we were too young to comprehend our own worth. He recognized this same heavenly investment within both Moses and Jesus long before the world ever saw it. They played pivotal roles, divinely appointed to bring salvation, hope, peace, joy, healing, and everything in between to God's people. They were carrying the very atmosphere of Heaven within them. The treasures within their spiritual boxes were priceless—and the devil knew it.

The enemy sought to kill these key players solely because of the roles they were going to be playing in this world's system. Now, we will never be asked to do what Jesus did because we all know Jesus was the ultimate sacrifice once and for all (Hebrews 10:1–18). Nor will most of us be called to deliver a group of Israelites from Egypt and split the Red Sea. However, one thing is for sure: any work for our Lord Jesus Christ is a direct threat to the enemy! This is why we see extremely early assassination attempts on so many of God's children's lives.

Now that we have covered a couple of biblical accounts of such attacks, I would like to dive right into the meat of this book. It is time to pull back the curtain and expose the enemy's hand in my own life. I will now share personal testimonies of assassination attempts I have dealt with that include physical, mental, and spiritual attacks. Many were plots and schemes from the enemy disguised as "accidents." The enemy does not care how he kills the children of God; he just desires to accomplish his mission to prevent us from fulfilling God's ultimate plans.

The first assassination attempt happened when I was an infant. In the winter of nineteen seventy-four, my family was taking one of many road trips to Missouri to visit my mom's family when I was just a few months old. We were driving across state lines in an old nineteen sixty-eight four-door Chevy Impala. Back in those days, there were no laws requiring parents to place their children in car seats, so my mother was holding me on her lap, and my sister and brother were in the back seat.

My dad decided to stop in a small town for gas and to allow everyone to stretch their legs. When my brother got out of the vehicle, there just so happened to be a soldier on duty from the United States Army who was filling up with gas at the pump next to us. He noticed that my brother was staggering as he got out to walk to the restroom. Recognizing that my brother was too young to be drunk, he alerted my dad that something was wrong. The soldier proceeded to tell my dad that he may have inhaled carbon monoxide poison by it seeping into our vehicle. He shared that recently several of the army trucks had experienced these similar types of leaks, and soldiers riding in them had displayed this same behavior.

After realizing what was going on, my parents frantically ran to check on my sister, who was still in the back seat. They remembered she had been very quiet on the last part of the trip, and she was still so little. When they opened her door, they discovered she was unconscious! She had succumbed to the poisonous fumes that had leaked inside. They quickly pulled her out and began trying to resuscitate her. After working on her for a good while, she finally regained consciousness.

However, as an infant, I was the most vulnerable of all the children because my body was the smallest. Yet God was looking after me and my entire family that night in a strange way. It just so happened that my mother had been smoking a cigarette as she held me in her arms, and she had cracked the small wing window open, allowing just enough air to circulate around my face, sparing me from the lethal effects. Now, some may discount that as coincidence, but I do not! I know it was a divine intervention by God to have that wing window open and the soldier at that gas station at the perfect time! God works and protects his children in mysterious ways. I can honestly say this was the only time I have ever thanked God for my mama smoking.

The second assassination attempt happened when I was three years old in the form of another accident. My sister and I were playing out in the backyard. I wandered off and found something that drew me away and caught my eye—a big barrel full of water! I ended up inside the barrel filled with water, in no time.

Thankfully, my sister saw me fall into the barrel and quickly ran inside for help. My mother came out like a bolt of lightning, running full speed ahead to help pull me out. Now, my mama has always been small and petite; she is about five feet one inch and never weighed much at all. I, on the other hand, was the opposite because I took after my dad's side of the family. Remember, I did say I was the family's chunky monkey. So, trying to get me out was not an easy task for such a small woman—especially considering she found me lodged headfirst inside this water barrel!

Our dad was seldom at home because he worked so hard to provide for the family, so my little mama was all on her own with this one. She said she had to struggle and struggle before she was able to finally set me free from that barrel. She was not sure how long I had actually been underwater before she was able to rescue me. Either way, my mother's relentless determination and mother's love paid off. A mother's determination can go a long way when one of her children's lives is at stake. My mother always said that without my sister being there and acting quickly, I would have died that day. I thank God for giving my sister the godly instinct to run and get help the way he did.

Another attempt took place when I was in elementary school, when my teenage brother decided that we were going to take a trip to the local corner store in his little orange Datsun truck. I remember him always loving to show off in front of all the neighborhood friends, and he would drive like a maniac to impress them, thinking he was Evel Knievel in the flesh. There was no law to wear seatbelts, so I was not constrained, and it had been raining like cats and dogs that day. The roads were very dangerous, wet, and slick.

As we approached the corner store, he was going too fast for the sharp turn and lost control of the truck as it went into a fishtail, sliding all over the slick road. Suddenly, the passenger door flung open with a huge gust of wind, and my body was now hanging out of the truck. I could feel the cold wind and rain hitting my face as I stared straight down into the black asphalt with my head just inches away from touching the pavement.

All of a sudden, I felt my brother's hand. I could not see his face, of course, because I was looking at nothing but concrete at this point, but I knew he was there because I felt his hand grab hold of my arm and attempt to pull me back into the truck. I still remember the feeling of knowing his hand was there and the relief that came over me at that instant. My brother was trying his best to get the vehicle back under control and pull me up simultaneously. In the process, I felt like I was being stretched like a rubber band that was about to snap in two pieces. He kept pulling and jerking me back and forth.

Finally, with a great surge of strength, I felt a last, final, hard jerk as my body flew back into the vehicle with a big thud. I did not know then, but I do know now, that God is the only one who could have given him such supernatural strength to pull me back in safely without wrecking us both in that vehicle. We could have easily gone out into eternity that day—but God!

The next attempt happened when I was about nine years old. My parents seldom allowed us to stay the night with our friends in hopes of protecting us from evil predators. So, when we did get the chance to spend the night with someone, it was always a fun experience. One summer, we got that chance with our good friend Holly. Her dad, Jim, lived in an apartment complex, and Holly would come down each summer to visit him. We always looked forward to it because they had a swimming pool. That equaled gold in our eyes!

When we arrived at the pool that day, I jumped into the pool and did not realize the depth of the water! Suddenly, as my head bobbed up, I realized my feet could not touch the bottom. I was way over my head, and I panicked! I began flailing my hands and feet as I desperately tried to come up for air. I remember screaming for help and inhaling a mouthful of water at the same time. After bobbing around, gasping for air, and going back under several times, that is when I felt a hand come down. Jim's strong hands suddenly grabbed my waist and pulled me out. Again, had it not been for God sending intervention right then, I would not be here today.

There were many other times throughout my teen years when God spared my life as well, and I will share some of those later in the book. You may be asking, how were those attempts on your life from the enemy? The enemy is a master of disguise, often masking his assassination attempts as mere "accidents." He loves to hide behind the veil of natural events to keep us ignorant of his true devices.

He loves to put thoughts in our minds, without us realizing it, to persuade us to do certain things, especially when we are young and defenseless. Too often, we are unaware that the outcomes and consequences of these choices are nothing more than a death sentence waiting to happen. Now, sometimes it is our own foolishness and flesh, but there are other times when it is absolutely a setup from the pits of hell. We must discern the difference.

Recently, precious pastor friends, Brooke and Beaux Jones, shared a similar account of these types of demonic plots with me. She and her family have experienced many witchcraft assignments sent in an attempt to attack them. They were living on a large piece of property at the time, and all the children knew not to go to the creek in the backyard. They had been told a hundred times, and they never went out to the creek.

However, one day, her young boy went missing. He was about three and a half years old at the time. They began to yell his name, frantically searching for him, and saw him afar off, walking toward the creek they had always warned the children to stay away from. Right before the little boy was preparing to get into the water, a family member safely grabbed him. She began asking him, 'Why did you try to go to the creek when we told you not to?' He told her that his half-sister, whom he had not seen in over a year, was bidding him to come join her in the creek.

The half-sister was a practicing witch who had been caught several times astral projecting into their home. This was no accident at all; it was an intentional setup to attempt to drown their little boy. Another time, there was another family member she attempted to seduce in the home. This young man was no blood-related to that side of the family; therefore, he had never met her and did not know what she looked like. When he walked into the bedroom, the woman was lying on his bed with no clothes. She did this several times to the husband and sons in the house, appearing either naked or wearing lingerie.

Later, they just happened to be looking at the family photo album when he saw the picture of the woman he had seen lying naked on his bed that day. It was the half-sister who had attempted to drown her half-brother. We will talk more concerning witchcraft later in this book, but I wanted to share this to show that just because things appear to be accidents, it means absolutely nothing when we are dealing with demonic spiritual warfare.

The enemy loves to cover things up with what appear to be natural events. The enemy is very cunning, and we must educate people so they are not ignorant of his devices. Second Corinthians 2:11: "Lest satan should get an advantage of us: for we are not ignorant of his devices."

However, for now, I want to share my next near-death experience when I was in my late thirties and a single mother. I had been extremely busy working at a car dealership, pushing myself far beyond my limits. All of a sudden, I began getting random phone calls from friends telling me they had been having dreams of me dying. Because of the amount of phone calls and random people confirming the same story, one even being an enemy, I slowly caught on to the fact that God was actually trying to warn me.

One morning, I woke up feeling extremely tired and weak. I forced myself to sit up anyhow, then tried to walk to the restroom. Suddenly, I felt I was going to pass out. I yelled for my daughter to come help me back to the bed, but before we reached the bed, I passed out cold and hit my face on the hard edge of the bed. When I awoke, I was lying in a puddle of blood. I noticed my cell phone had been going off—two different minister friends had sent text messages with encouraging Bible verses about God being a present help in trouble. Psalm 46:1: "God is our refuge and strength, a very present help in trouble."

I ended up at the doctor's office with black eyes and a busted nose. They ran tests and called me the next day, telling me to get to the hospital as soon as possible for a life-and-death emergency. My sister drove me, and the doctor explained that I had barely any blood left in my body. They had to do an emergency blood transfusion or I would die. The doctor was amazed at how I had been functioning. After the transfusion, I felt like a new woman! My life was spared by those who had the dreams and prayed, and by the doctors and donors God used.

The devil was constantly after me, trying to kill me any way he could to get to the treasures within my spiritual box. He was trying to stop me from sharing them with the world. Yet his best will never be good enough! I am convinced that God wants to use each one of us in his kingdom. He gives each of us these precious jewels from Heaven—the nine spiritual gifts, the fruit of the Spirit, wisdom, and love. Galatians 5:22–23: "But the fruit of the Spirit is love, joy, peace, long-suffering, gentleness, goodness, faith, meekness, temperance: against such there is no law." God designs each person according to his specific calling! We all have a purpose, a testimony, and a role to play. Welcome to the Treasures within Paula's Box. Step into the next few chapters with me as I open up my life and share the priceless jewels the Lord has hidden within.

Grandma Quick
(L) My sister & (R) Myself

GOING TO CHURCH
Maybe once a year

The Church my grandfather and great uncle built for the women to preach in.

Pastors:
Beaux and Brooke Jones

CHAPTER TWO

INVASION OF THE SOUL

I am the youngest in my family, and I have a brother eight years older than me and a sister just seventeen months older. My mother said raising us girls was like having twins, bless her heart. I can only imagine what she went through trying to raise us. I felt that my sister was the only one who had somewhat of a normal childhood and was always that smart kid who never really got into much trouble.

Our brother and I were unfortunately two totally different stories. I would like to share in this chapter how my brother's choices affected me especially, but also the entire family. He reminded me of a wild bull that nobody was able to tame, living with far less parental discipline than my sister and I. He seemed to do whatever he desired, but I truly believe the enemy worked overtime on his life for one reason: to prevent the mighty calling God has placed on him from ever materializing. He stayed in some kind of trouble, whether it was with the school, the neighbors, our parents, or even the law. I have no idea where his troubled roots stem from, but he definitely battled with some demons.

One incident that affected me growing up was the time he was severely attacked by a gang in Houston, where we lived. I have no clue what the fight was over; all I know is it was a bad fight. They had taken a baseball bat with nails protruding out of it and beaten him with it. He came home with both legs punctured and oozing blood all over the place. As a young child, it was so frightening to see what they had done to my brother and to be amid all that chaos that night. I remember him screaming in pain and cussing my parents in a state of delirious rage, losing himself entirely. No cops were called, and no police reports were filed either. At one point, my brother started learning karate and martial arts—I guess so they would not catch him off guard again and he could better defend himself. During this time, he would use my sister and me as his personal punching bags, trying his new maneuvers on us every time he learned one. We did not enjoy that at all, but I think that was his way of releasing all his pent-up anger and aggression. I guess at least he was learning self-defense, and we were learning how to toughen up.

When he got a little older, perhaps in his twenties, he and one of his buddies broke into our local convenience store to steal jewelry from the front display. I can only assume they planned to sell it to support their bad habits. But they got caught and were arrested. I remember visiting my brother in the county jail back then. I thought it was just terrible that my brother was locked up behind bars and away from home. Being so young, it was hard for me to understand what I perceived at the time as cruel punishment. And even worse, while awaiting trial, my brother's case was assigned to one of the toughest judges in Texas, known all over the state. I still remember sitting in the courtroom and sobbing on the day of his trial because my heart was broken for my brother having to be locked up behind those steel bars. It was hard to grasp the fact that he could be going away to prison for many years.

Although my mom was a preacher's kid and had been raised right in the church, she had stopped attending because of the spiritual abuse she witnessed over the years. However, one thing I noticed about my mama was the fact that whenever she found her children in trouble like she was experiencing at this time, she knew how to get hold of God. She remembered what she had been taught growing up. So, during this court case, she broke down once again and got hold of the hem of Jesus's garment on my brother's behalf (Matthew 9:20–22). On the day of the court hearing, to everyone's disbelief, the judge allowed my brother off with a slap on the wrist, and he served very little time. He was given one of the lightest sentences they had ever seen. The attorney and everyone in the courtroom was in shock as they heard the verdict. It was a sweet victory for our family and especially our brother!

At one point my brother decided to join the church that my aunt had attended. He gave his heart to the Lord and met a woman at the church who later became his wife. Unfortunately, a few years after getting saved, he fell away from God and started backsliding into a life of sin and chaos again. I remember seeing him being extremely hard on his children many times. I also recall walking into his home countless times when the entire house was filled with the aroma of weed. He was always drinking, fighting, doing drugs, or causing some kind of commotion. I believe he was trying to cope with internal pain and fell into substance abuse to mask the suffering he was dealing with. As you will see later in this book, I did the same.

One night he got into a heated argument with my parents when he was at our house with his two children. I was still young and in school, but I was helping babysit his children before he got there. When he came into the house, they all walked into my parents' room, across the hallway from mine. I could hear my mom, dad, and brother going back and forth, yelling at each other and cussing. I had no clue what was going on, but I figured he was high on drugs again. I grabbed his two children, and we hunkered down in my bedroom closet to hide. I was trying to calm them down and comfort them because they were crying hysterically. I needed them quiet so he would not find us and do something crazy.

The screaming and yelling intensified as the argument escalated, and soon it was obvious that there was a physical altercation more intense than any of the ones I had seen before. I heard things knocking over and banging going on. Then suddenly, I heard my mom and dad yelling at my brother, "Let go of the gun!" I really began to freak out at that point. I could not see what was going on, but I knew they were struggling over my daddy's gun. All of us knew where daddy kept the guns. I figured at any moment that gun was going to go off and kill my mom, dad, or brother. I was frightened and very concerned for everyone in the house.

Something I have noticed about myself over the years is that when I am in a fight-or-flight situation, I usually end up doing the unthinkable by standing up amid the evil. But in my panic, I was torn between leaving his frightened children alone or intervening between them. Impulsively, I jumped up and ran into my parents' room where they were struggling over the gun and screamed at the top of my lungs like a maniac, "Shut the F---up!" Now mind you, I had never cursed in front of my parents or yelled at them in any such manner. When I yelled, I felt everyone was stunned and caught off guard. There was a pause that had taken place in mid-action as they all stopped for a split second to look in my direction!

Literally, that split second gave my dad just enough time to snatch the gun from the clutches of my brother's hands, and he was able to gain full possession of the firearm again. I am certain it was the Spirit of God who came over me with the courage to react as I did. Of course, the curse word was not of God, but a direct manifestation of my own panicked flesh. I am referring to the boldness that came over me to leap into action and confront the situation, even in the midst of the fear. I am so thankful that night ended on a good note, and I thank God nobody died!

I remember another time when I was in high school, and my brother decided he wanted to kill his wife. She was at church on a Wednesday night, and my brother was convinced she was having an affair with the pastor's son. I found out he had told his friends about his plans that night to kill her. I remember pleading with my mom to go to the church and warn her, but she dismissed me, assuming he would eventually simmer down, and that he was just perhaps venting. So, I pleaded with her again, and despite my repeated cries for assistance, she refused. Finally, with utter boldness driving me, I stood up and threatened that if someone did not go, I would walk into that church and warn her myself. Now, the church she attended was a great Holy

Ghost-filled church, but because of the power of God there, I was scared to death to step foot inside of it. (I had visited the church years prior and had run out in fear; I will share that story in the next chapter.) However, regardless of my fears, I felt it was my duty to warn my sister-in-law. I felt someone had to drive to that church before she got home and ended up dead! Thankfully, after my strong threats, she finally listened, and I did not have to go after all. Shortly after this deranged incident, his wife left him and took their children with her to Louisiana.

I also recall at one point my brother becoming paranoid and delusional, thinking the FBI and the US Marshals were after him. I am sure he was high on drugs and demons were given legal access to hijack his mind again. At first, I thought he was for real and people were outside our home, but nobody was there. Hearing this and watching him go into this manic episode of panic, scared me. He literally thought they were hiding in our backyard, and he was scared out of his wits. He was hiding and yelling, telling us they were coming for him. He battled a lot of demons throughout his lifetime, causing our family a lot of hardships. He never had a normal life growing up. That is why I wanted to expand on his life briefly, because his life affected ours from day one. This is not to bash my brother at all, because I truly love him from the bottom of my heart. I just wanted to share a few of the cycles of attacks in his life and how the enemy tried to destroy him because of the treasures within his own personal treasure box—and how the enemy tried using him to affect the family.

I would have to say, though, the worst thing my brother put me through happened when I was in elementary school. He chose to hearken to the voice of satan one more time, who used him to molest me. I remember after he would molest me, he would instill fear into me by threatening me that I had better not breathe a word to anyone—especially our parents! This kept going on for a good while. I felt so torn and unclean, and I really wanted to tell my mom about what was happening, but I was scared to death of my brother and what he would do to me. When I finally decided to break my silence and tell my mother what had been taking place, she asked me multiple detailed questions, and I answered all of them honestly. I know they must have spoken to my brother after that, because the molestation immediately stopped.

But about a week after telling my mom, I can still remember, very vividly, the bitter sting of insult added to my injury. I had walked into the bathroom, watching my mama curl her hair in the mirror. I went to give her a kiss, as I had often done in the past. However, this time, I experienced one of the worst kinds of rejection I had ever known. She looked straight into my eyes and said, "I am not kissing you! I do not know where your lips have been!" As a small child, I was absolutely devastated. Her tone was cold—it did not even sound like my mom. It made me feel as if it was all my fault that my brother had done this to me. I had opened my heart to her, expecting understanding, but instead, her words hit my heart like a burning arrow. How could this be? She was the one who loved me more than anyone; she doctored me when I was hurting and protected me from harm's way. She had never been the one who struck out at me in such a ruthless manner, so I did not expect this type of pain from her. That arrow pierced deep, staying alive and on fire for many decades.

Looking back now, I wondered if she may have been trying to use reverse psychology on me, thinking if she said this, I would never allow him or anyone else to do such things to me again. Or perhaps it was the enemy who used her to say something hurtful to cause more pain to my already wounded heart, from the one I loved most. I honestly do not know why she said it, but I do know from that moment on, there was a dirty and shameful feeling that swept over my soul, and it stayed there.

So, needless to say, this incident with my brother had long-lasting effects on my mind. There were other times I was sexually abused as well, but my brother's act served as the open portal—a door in the spirit realm that was flung wide and stayed open, as pure evil would later begin to unleash against me.

I realize now that the enemy was trying to destroy my brother, and he was trying to use my brother to destroy me. But praise be to God, what the enemy intended for a death blow, the Lord turned it around for the good. While the enemy used my brother's hands to harm my body and break my spirit, God was using that fire to forge a 'godly toughness' I did not know I possessed. What was meant to break me would be the very thing God used to make me. I do not fault my brother for what happened because I know it was not my brother. Ephesians 6:12 He was purely being used by the enemy and heeded the wrong voice at that time. I love my brother very much, and I am so thankful for the relationship we have today. I am still praying and believing that one day my brother will surrender fully to Christ's plan because again I know he has a powerful calling on his life.

As I close this chapter, I must be honest with you: the shadows were only beginning to lengthen. The shame that was added to my life was about to be met by a storm of greater demonic obscurity. We are about to enter a season where the enemy did not just knock at the door;

he busted it down, moved in, and began a six-year siege of my innocence and for my very soul. Let us move into the next chapter—not because the truth is easy, but because the silence must be broken. It is time to take a stand and overcome by the blood of the Lamb and the Word of our testimony (Revelation 12:11).

Houston Revival Temple
Apostles Gene and Lorine Doyle

Mama and me

CHAPTER THREE

THE PUPPET MASTER'S PLAN

Now I realize I have mentally blocked out a lot of my past, so I will be sharing the parts of my testimony I can remember. Please know that, when I refer to demonic activity in this chapter, I literally mean demonic activity from demons, because the Bible is very clear in Ephesians 6:12, "For we wrestle not against flesh and blood, but against principalities, against powers, against the rulers of the darkness of this world, against spiritual wickedness in high places." It is not actually the people we are fighting, but it is the demons who use them as puppets to try to harm us.

After my brother molested me, as I mentioned, this opened many doors for this activity in my life. It felt as if I was walking around with a target on my back that only the kingdom of darkness could see. I did not realize then that the enemy uses the trauma we did not ask for to claim us as his own territory later. In this chapter, I am going to do my best to share those experiences with you. I began to deal with more encounters where the demons would entice other men to pick up the assignment of sexual abuse in my life, where my brother had left off. This often happens with abuse victims, but they do not know why. It is all part of spiritual warfare and attempts to destroy us.

One of the earliest memories I had of demonic activity being drawn around me like a magnet happened when my aunt took me to a carnival. I was about eight years old, and I was on a carnival ride that sat low to the ground and this ride would zigzag back and forth across the pavement. This old man, who was probably in his late fifties, began sticking out his tongue at me each time the ride passed him. Yes, back then someone in their fifties was extremely old to me. I had no clue why he kept doing this, but he just kept sticking out his nasty tongue and making unclean sexual gestures toward me. My aunt did not know what was going on because she could not see him from where she was standing. I did not understand why this old man did that, and his eyes looked like a ravenous wolf. I was petrified! Now, looking back, I know it was just part of that demon squad the enemy had sent out after to attack me and try to destroy me. As I mentioned in the first chapter of this book, the enemy tries in different ways to destroy people, and sexual predators are definitely one of his favorite ways. As I grew a little older, that demonic draw did not fade; it just switched faces. The enemy will use any open vessel that will allow him to.

I saw this clearly with a man who would stop by my parents' house from time to time. He worked behind our home at a small family business and always seemed well-mannered. He was probably twenty-five years old very clean-cut and nice-looking. I always thought he looked like Tom Cruise. He put on a good front before everyone with his clean-cut image, and my parents trusted him. Little did I know underneath that clean-cut image sat a predator waiting for my parents to look away. One day he asked my parents if he could drive me to the local 7-Eleven to buy me a Slurpee and they said yes, not even stopping to think twice. I was excited to get to go to the corner store for a Slurpee, but had no clue he had other motives in mind that day. On that trip he molested me as well. He was forcefully kissing me, had his hands down into my pants and over my breasts. Of course, like all predators, he instilled fear and threatened me not to say anything. As victims tend to do, I did not open my mouth about the events of that day. It was as if the enemy was marking me, layer by layer, proving that the spiritual magnet was pulling the worst kind of people into my path.

I also recall the enemy using my girlfriend's dad, who was another puppet for that demonic draw. He always made creepy and lustful remarks towards me each time I saw him. I was extremely uncomfortable around him and knew something was not right about him. He would make perverted comments and tell me how "hot and sexy my lips looked". With him being the same age as my father or older, this made me want to vomit. I loved hanging out with my friends but would stay away on purpose to avoid visiting because of her dad. It wasn't until years later that I discovered he had been molesting my girlfriend and her sister for their entire lives. I am so glad that I listened to my gut instincts and chose not to go around them anymore. To this day, I feel they are both mentally unstable because of his abuse—a direct result of the enemy's plan to destroy innocent lives. Oh, how I pray they will one day receive healing from Jesus, just as I have, so they too can experience mental stability and peace in their lives.

I was leaving elementary school and preparing to enter junior high, carrying a lot of emotional baggage. That weight was about to get much heavier as I entered one of the deepest, darkest seasons of my life; it was as if the enemy was preheating his demonic oven.

As I started the sixth grade, I found my first boyfriend and what many would call their "first love." I met him on a CB radio, which was our substitute for social media back in those days. My boyfriend's name was Larry, and he was five years older than me. I had no idea when we first met that he was extremely controlling, manipulative and violent. Nor did I know anything about a relationship, and this one became extremely toxic straight out of the gate. I think the only reason my mother liked and allowed me to date him was because she figured he would keep an eye on me. To her, he was a babysitter, boyfriend, and dad all in one who would keep me safe from harm. But she did not know the true deity that controlled him from behind his mask of the flesh.

The puppet master would take him over regularly, pulling his strings ever so strategically to inflict his cruel venom into my life. Of course, I knew nothing about spiritual warfare back then or what was really going on until I had become saved decades after this. If I made him mad, he would explode like a stick of dynamite and start punching walls, vehicles, doors, and whatever else was in his path during his tantrum. He would hit things that were very close physically near my face, screaming at me, "See what you make me do, Paula! This is all your fault!" I felt he wanted to show his dominance, showing me he could easily land one of those punches on my face. One day he tried doing exactly that! We had gotten into a big fight when I found out that he was sleeping with the girl down the road again.

When I went down to her house intending to fight her, he saw me and came running down the street like a man possessed by legends. His face contorted with a rage as it often did when he got mad. That is when he threw a punch straight at my face. Thankfully though, his best friend, Chris, was there, who jumped in between us and caught his punch in midair when his fist was just inches away from my face! I had never seen a punch intercepted like that except on TV. I was ever so very thankful for Chris that day, and looking back, I feel he was another person sent by God to intervene in my life to protect me. In our circle, people knew Chris as the Ninja because he trained as a mixed martial artist. Chris was a great guy, but he was to be feared when it came to fighting. Everyone knew not to mess with Chris, and that included his best friend, Larry.

Larry always wanted me right by his side so he could know exactly what I was doing around the clock. He loved to control me, and he was successful at doing just that for many years. However, one weekend he must have gotten a wild hair because he allowed me to hang out with my best friend, Stephanie. I believe he only let me go because he was cheating and did not want me messing up the game he was running. He was always with different girls, but nevertheless, I was thrilled for the rare chance to be away from him. I felt like a free animal finally stepping out of the cage he kept me locked up in. This night there were two parties right by each other. One was at my friend Renea's house, and the other one was at my friend Angela's house. The houses were close, only a block away from each other. Stephanie told me to stay at Renea's house and, when I finished at that party, to meet her at Angela's. She did not know my friend Renea very well and wanted to stay at Angela's most of the night. After finishing Renea's party, I began to walk to Angela's house. It was dark, but I thought nothing of it because I was not that far away from the house, but as I walked down to the second party, two guys from my class at school approached me. They began a casual conversation and inquired where I was going. I thought it was odd; they did not seem to know about the two parties when I told them. They both lived in the area and knew both girls who were having the parties that night because we all went to school together. I had no reason to fear them, but the spiritual target on my back was evidently glowing in the dark. Because out of nowhere, I was thrown into a big, deep ditch that was on the side of the road. One got on top of me, straddling me, and ripping my shirt open to fondle my breasts, while the other was digging through my purse and throwing my belongings out in the ditch. I can still remember hearing them laughing as they were doing all this and speaking in Spanish to one another. I have no clue what they were saying or why on earth they were even doing this, because these were guys from my class. Every day, I would see them as I sat by them in school. As we struggled, I was screaming for help and trying to fight the one guy off, but he was too strong and had the upper hand. Then, speaking in English, the guy named Jose, who was on top of me, told me, "This is what happens to girls like you." I knew his intention was to rape me right there. I struggled for several minutes trying to fight him off, to no avail. Then, suddenly, simultaneously, both guys jumped up out of the ditch and ran off. It was as if they had seen a ghost or something! They both bolted out as quickly as they had come in! I have no clue what happened. All I knew is that they had disappeared. I would like to think, perhaps, they saw an angel. Whatever they saw was enough to stop the enemy's plan dead in its tracks. But you know how the enemy loves to salt a wound; he was not finished emptying the shaker. Instead of being able to find comfort after such a terrifying night and the great interception that transpired, destroying the plot of satan, I found myself trapped between the trauma of the ditch and the terror of Larry's temper.

I did not know how to handle the situation! Telling my boyfriend terrified me, given what might happen to me or those boys. He stayed looking for a fight with anyone at any time, and I walked on eggshells trying to keep the serpent tamed from striking. He would go unhinged and out of control over minor issues, so this would have definitely caused a trigger. I decided to remain silent. However, over the years I have learned a lesson that a shut mouth can lead to worse situations later! If you are going through something like this, please do not keep your mouth shut, like I did! If they do it to you, they will do it to the next innocent person as well! Often, the longer the person goes unreported, the longer the demon is allowed to operate through the person, and the attacks will only get worse as time goes by. If you wait to report it today, the victim of tomorrow may not be alive with a voice to report it with. Also, you will find there is healing and freedom in reporting it to someone and getting help.

The following Monday after this attack, when it was time to go back to school, these boys totally humiliated me again. (As if the first time was not bad enough!) I did not want to face them, but I knew I could not skip school. Remember, I did not report the attack out of one of satan's best weapons he used on me so often, the spirit of FEAR! In our class there was another

Hispanic boy who had been so nice and kind towards me. He did not seem to be like the other guys in the class, and would speak to me every day, saying hello with a warm smile on his face. He genuinely seemed to be a good-hearted guy and so much to the point, I considered him a friend. However, I quickly learned this so-called "friend" was actually no friend at all and did not differ from them. The day I returned to class, both the boys from the weekend were sitting at their desks just staring and laughing at me. They then began to talk in Spanish to the other boy; I had considered my friend for so long. I noticed my "friend" quickly glanced over at me, then joined in their jesting and was laughing right along with the two boys. Of course, I have no clue what exactly they said, but I know it had something to do with what they had done to me in the ditch.

My life was a mess. I was already dealing with a psychotic, abusive boyfriend and now undergoing this degradation, things just kept getting worse for me. My boyfriend was not only verbally abusive and terrorizing, but he was also sexually abusive. I was only twelve at the time and having sexual intercourse with him. He would drive me every morning into the wooded area behind my middle school to have sex with me before school would even start. He would do things to me sexually that I never knew even existed. These are the memories I have always tried to forget because they carry such heavy pain whenever they come to mind. He would do extremely demented and sadistic sexual acts on me, treating me like a sex slave or a sexual science project. With every detail, he insisted that I reenact the pornographic scenes he had watched. He would handcuff me, tie me up, burn candle wax over my genitals, insert foreign objects that do not belong in the human body, using harmful chemicals to penetrate me, bite me leaving marks, choke me, etc.

There were many times I would physically pass out in the middle of these sexual acts. All this was going on at twelve years old. He subjected me and my body to acts that most fifty-year-old women have never performed in their marriage beds–acts that should never be done to a human's body under any circumstances! It was just pure evil and sadism. Now the question arises: why would I stay and put up with that? I truly believe it was because of the fear he imparted to me at such an early age. I feel I developed what most psychologists call Battered Woman Syndrome with PTSD. This starts a cycle of fear in your life and causes you to stay with your abuser when you should have left long ago. It is an extremely hard cycle to break, especially if you do not have a relationship with the Lord Jesus Christ.

Besides, when we would get into a fight and I would say I wanted to leave, Larry would threaten to kill me. He would always say those famous words, "If I can't have you, nobody will."

I did not realize at the time, but do now, he was bound by an unclean spirit of sexual addiction that no one woman would be able to quench because this was a spiritual battle, not a human one. One time at the beginning of the relationship, before I realized he had been unfaithful, he told me he had got crabs, and I literally thought he meant that he went fishing. I had no idea what crabs were or how they were caught. He explained to me what they were but told me he had gotten them from trying on clothes at the store. I was so young; I did not know any better and believed him! Thank God, he never transmitted them to me!

However, years later I did contract two sexually transmitted diseases because of his secretive and vile lifestyle he led. However, thank God, medicine easily treated them, and the doctor gave me a full clean bill of health after the treatment concluded. The man was sick in so many ways and had many demons. Even after catching him cheating regularly, I still felt I could do nothing about it because I was so scared!

While I was dating Larry, I began to take on his demons. Yes, that can happen. Demons can jump from one person to the next just like those nasty crabs he caught. I began doing things that were totally out of character for me. My heart and mind were turning dark, just like his had always been. I began to do off the wall things, and stealing was one of them. I remember one time going to a gas station where one of Larry's friends worked, but he was not on duty that night. Larry's friend knew how the gas pump system worked and how to turn it off and on. So, Larry and his friend gave me and my friend instructions to go inside the store and flirt with the clerk to distract him. As we were distracting the clerk, Larry's friend turned on the pump, and they all pulled their vehicles around to fill their gas tanks up. I do not recall how many vehicles got a full tank of gas that night, but there were several. I cannot even fathom how much of a loss that owner took in fuel and what the outcome was for the clerk who was working in the store.

On another occasion, we were in Humble, Texas and Larry and his crew saw cases of soft drinks stacked outside as a display near the mall. We all loaded up the back of Larry's truck, totally full of cases upon cases of soft drinks, and dropped them off at the party house where we all hung out. There were enough sodas to fill up two full refrigerators, from top to bottom. I was also very naïve about where he had been taking me all those years because, unbeknownst to me, that party house was a hub for drug deals and drug use. Once, someone even shot another person right outside the front door, in cold blood over a dispute.

Another time, some of my friends and I went shoplifting at Deerbrook Mall. We would casually slip items into our shopping bags or purses and walk out with them. I remember stealing a big neon light-up clock for absolutely no reason. My parents were not rich, but we did not go without. I feel I was doing it out of rebellion and I had been learning tricks from Larry and his petty theft lifestyle.

Once while we were shoplifting in Deerbrook Mall, we heard on the walkie-talkies the associates calling the mall security on us, and we ran before they could catch us. I often say the only difference between myself and some behind bars is that I did not get caught. I feel God knows who can handle being locked up and who cannot. God truly knew this girl could not handle a life behind bars. I am so grateful for His amazing grace that was looking out for me in my stupidity.

Another favorite spot we liked to hang out at was a place in Houston called Beltway and Rankin. This was a well-known hotspot where everyone went to party, drink and drag race. Everyone knew the cops would make their rounds every so often and do their bust, so we had to stay on the lookout. This one Saturday night, several of my friends drove their vehicles out there with Larry and me. My sister rode with another carload of people, but the driver took off down the road to cruise around and left them behind with us, planning on coming back for them after he circled around. However, before he had a chance to come back, the cops did a bust. So, we all had to take off and run to not risk going to jail.

However, my sister and her friend were stuck without rides because the guy had not yet made it back. Larry quickly told them all to get in and hide in the bed of his truck. He then pulled his bed cover down so nobody would see them. That is when we took off like something out of a Dukes of Hazard episode, running from the cops. We jumped a big ditch to get away, but as soon as we came up on the other side, there the officers sat on the opposite side of the road. Patiently waiting with their red and blue lights flashing, they sat there as if they had been expecting us the whole time. They made us exit the vehicle and began to ask Larry questions. They searched the vehicle and told Larry to lift the truck bed cover, and found everyone in the back. The police gave Larry and the other guy who was with us a hard time because they found wrappers in Larry's glove box, but no marijuana. Of course, I had always been told the wrappers and condoms in the glove box belonged to his best friend, Chris. He told me Chris asked him to keep them for him, and he was just doing what a real friend would do. I was so blinded by his lies that I believed him. Thankfully, they did not arrest any of us that night, called our parents and let us go.

Right after I turned thirteen, I found out I was pregnant with Larry's child. When I called him to tell him, he was heartless and cold towards me, and at that very moment he revealed he was cheating on me again. Of all times, this was not the time I needed to hear this. I began crying and screaming at him, telling him I could not believe he was doing this to me at a time like this! I will always remember the despair I felt when he so carelessly hung up on me. I was scared and felt I could not tell anyone and had no clue what to do. So, I just bottled it up along with everything else I had been dealing with. Then one day my mama came to me because she knew something was not right with me. She just point-blank asked me. "Paula, are you pregnant?" I broke down crying uncontrollably, telling her I had not had a cycle in at least five months. She immediately took me to an abortion clinic, with no questions asked. Larry was called by my mom and went with us as well. I was told I was having an abortion, and that was that. There were no ifs, and or buts about it. There was no discussion of a future with the baby or even consideration of putting the child up for adoption. Since I was so far along in the pregnancy, the doctors had to insert something inside me and told me to come back for the completion of the abortion. The sad fact of the matter is, I later learned they inserted objects in late-term abortions to break up the flesh of the baby, to make it easier to remove the babies for the doctors. So, they are cruelly butchering the unborn fetus inside the womb and then removing it. I still remember being under so much stress that day that I ended up having a seizure, knocking Larry in the head in the process, as they were driving me to the abortion clinic in the vehicle. Looking back, you might think they would have pulled the vehicle over or informed the doctor once we arrived; but they did not. Sadly, they performed the abortion that day, and Larry remained in the picture like the Black Plague he was.

After the abortion, my life crumbled and really spin out of control! I had now opened the door for even bigger demons, that intertwined with the ones I had taken on from Larry. Everything I had battled just seemed to intensify after killing my own child. I was so depressed! The drinking was off the chart! I relentlessly tried using alcohol in an attempt to numb my conscience and dull the pain. Yet, day after day, I still woke up to the same problems. I lived in a constant state of rage, getting into fights in the neighborhood, at school, and constantly finding trouble with the administrators. My mom encouraged me to fight as we were growing up, which did not help in this situation. It only reinforced and solidified in my mind that it was okay to take my anger out on others. I believe she wanted us to be tough as nails and able to hold our own, but there was a lack of limits to those methods. Mama would often make my sister, our friends, and I fight on the living room floor on Saturday nights, acting as the referee. I felt like this was her form of Saturday night entertainment, as she was trying to teach us life skills. She always instilled one rule in us: never start a fight, but if someone started one, we had to finish it. If not, she would whip us when we got home.

This was the reality I faced the day our neighbors across the street started provoking me into a fight. There were three of them outside staring me down: the big brother, the middle sister, and the youngest sister. The little sister was the one flapping her lips, though, and taunting me. My mom demanded that I go whip this girl and teach her a lesson. Mama would also instruct us to fight off other people's property; for legal purposes. I did not mind fighting the girl because I knew I could take her. However, she had backup that day, and I told my mom, "But there are three of them and only one of me." She replied, "You tell them you are only fighting her, then you pull her out by the hair of her head, drag her into the street, and take care of business. If not, I am going to whip you." Well, I was too scared not to obey what she said, because Mama did not play. She might have been little, but I knew she would make good on her promise. So, I did just as I was told, but they all jumped in instead. That is when I ended up having to fight all three at once. But at least I avoided a whipping from Mama.

I recall another time when a boy tried to put his books on my desk, and it made me mad. I thought to myself, who does he think he is? Does he not know whose desk this is? Without thinking twice and with no hesitation, I punched him right between his eyes. He fell backward; his glasses flew off, and onto the floor he went. I did not care if they were male or female; I was not discriminatory based upon gender. The spirits on me were equal opportunity agents that were having fun playing "Romper Room" with my mind. I was being used as one of the devil's many puppets, dancing to his strings to hurt others.

Then there was Dawna, a girl who kept running her mouth like a yapping Chihuahua. At least that is how I perceived her and the incident on that day. I had been in so much trouble from fighting that I was really trying to avoid any more detention, but one day, she poked the bear one too many times. I knew it was time to confront her and settle the score once and for all. As my friends and I were walking home, I tossed my books to a classmate, hiked up my long blue jean skirt, and the chase began. I bolted down the middle of the street, screaming at the girl who was now fearing for her very life. It appeared the once yapping Chihuahua had finally stopped barking and started crying. Though she had a good lead, I refused to let up, even when she plunged into the woods. I remained hot on her trail, tracking her like a bloodhound on a scent. By the time we were approaching our houses, she jumped over the bridge connected to her property. I knew then she was off-limits to me at that point, since she had reached her property line. Her dad came running out to her rescue, yelling, and a pretty heated argument escalated between my mom and her dad. He threatened to call the law on me and told my mom that she needed to get me under control. He was right; I was totally out of control. But Mama would not be the one to help keep me in line—only God could handle such a task. I find it ironic that I always wanted to dress nice and carry myself like a lady, yet I acted like a man—a lunatic fueled by rage.

Another fight that got me into the most trouble with the school system was with Jenzy. This one started because Jenzy said something about Larry. I asked my girlfriends to take her to a particular bathroom in the school. These girls were in a small gang, but I would never join them when asked. However, I was good friends with one of the gang leaders, so I asked her for a favor that day. I asked her to gather all the girls and ensure Jenzy moved into the restroom where I waited to attack her. The hallways were extremely crowded. As the girls shoved her into the restroom, she began to scream and jump up and down, pleading for the teachers' help. I was in the bathroom stall waiting and pretending to use the restroom, just in case a teacher came in. But when the teacher caught on to what was going on and rescued Jenzy, they found me hiding there. The teachers knew exactly what I was up to. They sent me to the principal's office and gave me all-day in-school suspension. We called it SAC back then. The principal told the SAC teacher not to allow me to leave the building when the last bell rang until all the other students had gone. I told the principal I had fought no one, and I would not pay a price for something I did not do. In my mind, I was being punished for no reason because I had not actually fought her yet. He knew I intended to get my revenge. As soon as the bell rang, I left the room; the teacher had forgotten the principal's instructions. I hauled out of that classroom as quickly as I could to look for Jenzy. As I opened the double doors to our temporary buildings, Jenzy was right there the moment they swung open. I immediately punched her one time. She fell backward, hitting the concrete slab as she landed. I did not stick around for anything else; I felt I had accomplished my mission. I ran out before any teachers could snatch me up again. Later, I heard reports that she was knocked unconscious on the concrete. My parents got a call a few hours later stating the girl was in the hospital with a concussion. They were threatening legal action against me.

There were countless more fights after this, and normally I would receive disciplinary actions resulting in a one to three-day suspension. The punishment for fighting Jenzy was much longer, though. Expulsion from that incident led to a two-month sentence, confining me at home rather than the typical three days. Instead of it being a punishment to me though, it was actually a vacation with me sunbathing in my backyard. My expulsion ended just days before our junior high prom. Months before the fight, I had already purchased a red, Southern-bell-style dress, and I was excited to wear it. That is when they called the police in to have a one-on-one conversation with me. They threatened me, saying they would be watching me at the prom that night, and if anything went down, they were hauling me off. I was snarky and completely disrespectful toward the officers, telling them she was not worth my time, nor was she worth messing up my hair and dress over.

Principals and staff members also held meetings to discuss sending me to an alternative school for bad children. It was during one of those meetings that they included my mom. When they told her what they were considering, she started welling up with tears in her eyes. I knew that only meant one thing: she was not sad as they had supposed but quite the opposite; she was now infuriated. She went off like the firecracker she was and told them I would absolutely not be doing any such thing. My mama would go to war for her children any day of the week, whether we were right or wrong. In this situation, I was completely in the wrong and utterly out of control. Yet, I was thankful for my mama fighting the school system, and she had won.

I still sparred with the enemy over my mind, even though I had won the battle with the school. The spirit of rage and anger was breathing down my neck daily. I had all these toxic emotions bottled up, and I was waiting to explode on anyone. I did not realize that when I had the abortion, there was an exchange that had taken place in the spirit realm. A door opened, allowing multiple demon spirits to come in and have a demonic party with my mind and emotions. I was battling daily with the spirits of murder, rage, depression, violence, suicide, shame, death and more.

On a couple of occasions, I attempted suicide by cutting my wrists and ingesting pills. I would always cut my arms with a knife or a razor blade to try to ease the mental anguish that I was battling. I felt the physical pain would help take my focus off the mental pain. However, I know now it was just a demonic tool the enemy used to cause me to self-destruct, just as suicide is. The enemy hates that God created us in His image and therefore tempts us to destroy our bodies with such devices. All the while eating in the back of my mind was the deep-rooted guilt I felt for the abortion. I did not know how to process nor how to escape it all, and the demons I was battling were getting stronger by the day.

I began drinking constantly. I would get extremely drunk. But my mama always had a rule for her kids: if you were going to drink, you were going to do it in her presence. So, we would have parties just about every weekend and get plastered sitting at the kitchen table. All the kids loved hanging out at our house for this very reason. One of these parties took place at our lake house my parents owned in Livingston after a spaghetti dinner. We were playing a game of quarters that requires you to bounce a quarter off the table and make it land in the shot glass. If you miss, you drink that shot. That night, I became completely intoxicated. I'm sure I had alcohol poisoning from drinking so much. Before this, I had been drunk many times, but I had never felt that sick from alcohol, ever. I kept throwing up over and over and could not stop. Before the night was over, my regurgitated plate of spaghetti ended up sitting on Larry's lap. I could not even walk. For hours, I dry-heaved, experiencing dizziness, dehydration, and difficulty breathing. I was still awake, dry heaving when the sun came up the next morning.

I started carrying alcohol in my water bottle to school and a switchblade in my purse just in case I needed to use it, compliments of Larry, of course. I would rather fight and take my anger out on another human than to look at them. I knew things were getting out of hand the day I caught Larry cheating on me again, and I started to plot out literally how I was going to murder the girl. I had decided I was going to wait until she left her house, hide in the bushes and stab her with the knife Larry had given me. My mind was warped, twisted, and sick, just like his had been from the first day we met.

One thing he did to me constantly that racked my nerves was screaming at me as the demons took him over. These tantrums would take place in private and in public. He would lose all control, screaming until the veins in his neck protruded, spitting in my face and accusing me of doing something wrong. It was pure humiliation to me because God only knows I was too scared to open my mouth and say something back to him. I felt I had to just take it from him, spit and all!

One summer break in my high school year, right before tenth-grade, we went to buy steaks at the Fiesta store off Airline Drive in Houston. Something set Larry off that day, and he began acting crazy towards me in the middle of the store, cussing me out. Then, when I went back to school a couple of months later, we switched to our new classes with a different teacher and new students. One of my classmates told me he recognized me and had seen me before. I was wondering where because I never recalled seeing this boy in my life. He explained he had seen me come into the Fiesta store where he was working. He told me I had been with an older guy who was tall, had dark hair and darker skin. He said, "The guy was yelling and cussing at you while you were standing by the meat counter." I could not believe this guy remembered me from months prior, but he said the scene Larry had made he had not forgotten. He was asking me if we were still together and had a shocked look on his face when I told him we indeed were.

Another burst of demonic manifestation broke out when he saw me driving in my neighborhood, after I had mentioned breaking up with him. He went full-blown berserk on me again. He was leaning out of his car window and screaming, demanding that I pull over. He was driving so erratically that I just knew we were about to collide. Afraid we would wreck; I pulled my car over. That is when he forcefully pushed his way through my car door, turned off the engine, and snatched my keys. He was screaming in my face—with those same veins popping out of his neck—and threatening to kill me if I ever left him. He did all of this in broad daylight in the middle of the street, as if he did not care who saw. To get my keys back, he made me swear right there in the road that I would never leave him. I ended up staying for six agonizing years! I had no clue how to end this relationship or how to tell anyone what was really happening behind closed doors.

My mind was shot by this time in my life, and I had become my abuser. The very things that I hated about Larry, I was doing myself. But six years later, I met a guy named Shawn. We started talking, and I could see that he was nothing like Larry.

He was extremely nice and treated me very well. The more I talked to Shawn, the more I liked him and enjoyed his company. I began to see him as often as I could when Larry went to work. My mom hated the idea of me seeing Shawn, though. She wanted only me with Larry. On the night of my birthday, I wanted to go see him and lied to my mom about where I was going, telling her I was going to my girlfriend's house. One thing you did not do was lie to my mom; she hated when people lied to her, and she had figured out somehow that I was lying about where I went that night. She got so upset with me; she threw a full bottle of champagne right at my head as I was walking out the door. Thank God, she missed me because had she not, it would have split my head in two.

I am not sure if she told Larry that night or if someone else told him that I had gone to visit Shawn, but he found out somehow. And that was when another devastating blow happened in my life by the hands of my abuser. One that would end up tormenting me while I was awake, asleep in my dreams, and around the clock in my thoughts. Larry snapped and took it to a level of abuse I had yet to endure. Even though I had dealt with a lot up to this already. Larry sodomized and raped me as my punishment when he found out I had been seeing Shawn. As I was screaming and begging him to stop, he pushed a pillow hard into my face to muffle my screams and refused to stop! He had done many terrible sexual things to me previously, but he had not gone this far before. However, that was the last straw for Paula. I could no longer endure another one of Larry's fits of rage or sexual abuse! I did not know how to get away from him, but that day I made up my mind that I was going to get away someway and somehow. So, I started coming up with craftier ways to avoid him. However, he had full access to my house, and they treated him like family, which made it difficult. I went to my mom and explained to her that I wanted to break up with him, but she did not understand. I am sure she thought we simply had another fight, because we fought all the time–it was our normal. Many nights I remember him sitting on the side of my bed, arguing with me as I was falling asleep, knowing I would have school the next day and needed to get to bed early. Often, I would pretend I had fallen asleep, playing possum, in hopes he would just leave. Some nights it actually worked, and other nights it did not. He would sit on the side of my bed arguing as I fell asleep, regardless!

As I previously mentioned, I do not think my mom wanted us to break up because he was my adult babysitter. She truly felt that he was protecting me because he loved me so much. Larry had a love for me alright, but it was a very dark, twisted kind of love. She did not realize he was killing me inside and that I had endured the abuse from him, that I had. She did not know how demonic and toxic this relationship had become. I finally got the courage to stand up and tell Larry I wanted out of the relationship, as well as my mom. I believe he knew all he had done to me had finally taken its toll on me. When I told my mom, she did something very odd and begged us to go to church with her. She kept pressuring us to go for some reason. This was extremely unlike my mother. After years of partying with her and only going to church once or twice a year for holidays, this did not make any sense. So, I thought maybe we should go after all. I thought surely there is a reason she is asking us to go so adamantly. So, for my mother's sake alone, I agreed to go to church with them. But in hindsight, I think she simply thought I was making a big mistake by breaking up with Larry, and this was her last-ditch effort and hope that God could perhaps keep us together if she just took us to church. Just like with my brother's court trial, when push came to shove, my mama knew God was real and that he answered her prayers–even if they were seasonal prayers from desperate situations.

So grudgingly, we went to what we called the Family Church, the same one where my brother met his wife, the same one I had visited in elementary school, and the same one my Aunt Myrtle was a part of and many other family members visited. So, I was sitting on this church pew full of mental anguish, confusion, hurt, and pain inside. I was one mentally messed-up girl, full of demons. There was an old man preaching that night named Rev. Billy Griffin. He went around the church telling people things that supposedly only God and they knew. Later I found out that was called prophecy. I was fascinated by all this and wondered if this was real–if this stuff could really be happening. So, I said in my head, "God, if you are real, have that man say something to me. Does this stuff really happen? Is this stuff true?" As soon as those words came to my mind, that old preacher came up to me and pointed his little bony finger in my face. He started yelling at the top of his lungs, as his head was bobbing back and forth like a wild man saying, "Sister, if you want it to happen, it will happen!" Boy, did that scare the living daylights out of me! I was tripping out because I did not know what to think about it all. Now mind you, God was just simply using this vessel to answer my question that I had just asked, but it terrified me! The answer from God happened so quickly and took me by surprise! Now, at this stage of the relationship, I knew Larry did not want me to break up with him, and I knew he would do anything to keep me. So, I turned to Larry and started whispering and cursing at him under my breath, saying, "Get the ^*#$ up and get out of this church!" I figured if he was the first one to get up, it would not make me look as bad. I had to repeat myself twice before he finally got up to walk out, but he eventually walked out. I still could not believe that incident happened, and that God answered me that quickly. I realized in that encounter there was a true higher power working behind that old man. But it shook and frightened me to my core; I never wanted to go back to that church again because of that incident. Except for the time I mentioned in the previous chapter when I felt someone needed to warn my sister-in-law about my brother who was going to kill her when she arrived home after church that night.

Attending a church service did not change my heart's desire to sever ties with Larry, as I suppose my mother was wishing for. The truth was, I was still working on letting him go for good, but I felt paralyzed. Resisting this demonic pull and breaking free from the soul tie binding me to him was something I wasn't sure how to do. I knew I could not deal with him anymore, but I was mentally messed up in the head and sick when it came to him. I would break up with him, and then he would draw me right back in, like a fish on a hook. However, not long after that encounter with God, I finally got bold enough to tell him again, I did not want to see him anymore! I told him to leave me alone. He did not take it too kindly and flew into another emotional whirlwind. I found myself in a high-speed chase with him that night down Aldine Bender Rd. He had a faster 5.0

Mercury Capri car, and I had a little 200sx 4-cylinder Nissan. As I was running from him, he got caught by a stoplight, and it gave me just enough time to pull into a little supermarket parking lot and quickly turn my headlights off, waiting for him to pass me by. But as he passed, he noticed my vehicle parked with no lights on and did a donut in the middle of the road and began to chase me again! I high-tailed it back to my house with the gas pedal all the way to the floor! I felt my safety would be assured once I reached my house. I figured if he was going to harm me, he would have to do it in front of my parents. I did something really stupid though and ran all the red lights on the way home just to get away from him. He was on my bumper the entire way and ran all the red lights right behind me! Our extremely dangerous driving and the way we ran those lights could have easily killed us. Or worse, we could have killed an innocent family. Can you say more of God's amazing grace? I pulled into my parent's driveway and ran quickly inside, demanding that my parents make him leave. They hesitated at first about what was going on and did not realize what had just happened with the high-speed chase. They had always allowed him to come over anytime he wanted, and proper boundaries had never been in place. This was another factor I had battled so much: the carte blanche access he seemed to have been granted and the control he had even gained in my own home. However, I steadily demanded that my parents make him leave! I told my parents they would either make him leave, or I would call the cops myself and the cops would. I had made up my mind, and I was not putting up with him anymore! They yielded to my request and made him leave. At last, the rollercoaster ride from the pits of hell was over!

Larry and me

Larry and me

CHAPTER FOUR

WHISPERS FROM THE WELL

Even though the relationship was over and I was physically free from Larry, mentally I was still his prisoner. I did not know how to live a normal life after that. When I went out with friends, I was constantly fearing he would pop up because we had so many mutual friends. Panic attacks became my new norm. If someone even mentioned his name, I would immediately begin shaking inside and out, get sweaty palms, and hyperventilate. I would have to talk myself off a mental rollercoaster of negative thoughts the enemy was feeding my mind. I would remind myself he was not there and tell myself, "I am safe, just breathe and calm down."

The battle did not end when the sun went down; the torment followed me into my sleep. Along with that paranoia, I had constant nightmares about him. I would wake up in cold sweats, riddled with fear, trying to catch my breath. I realized that my developing fear of men generally wasn't just caused by Larry's abuse. This feeling, I suspect, developed gradually because of the abuse I experienced from other men.

Despite my diligent efforts to uphold my "tough girl" persona, the spirit of fear would cause the mask to falter. I would have random panic attacks when I found myself around men, as if my body remembered a danger my mind was trying to forget. I once needed my tire repaired and had to go to a tire shop. As I sat in the tire shop lobby waiting on the repairs, I noticed I was drowning in a sea of men surrounding me, and the walls began to close in. The spirit of fear hit me so powerfully that I started to sweat, shake, and struggle for every breath.

I would have panic attacks around all kinds of men. However, I noticed when I came into close quarters with a Hispanic man, I would really see a flare-up take place. This was likely linked to the attack in the ditch, as both involved Hispanic men. I was afraid of Hispanic men for years afterward and avoided interacting at all costs. In fact, one time our neighbors were having their roof replaced, and a group of Hispanic men were on top of the roof working. My fear prevented me from going to check the mailbox at the end of our driveway. I whispered to myself, trying to anchor my emotions, telling myself I would not fear and I would be okay. I tried to use logic, asking myself, "What are they going to do—jump off the roof and run across the street?" Yet I still had to tell myself that I was a grown woman and I would not be a coward. But the mind and the body do not always agree. As soon as I made it to the mailbox, I had a full-blown panic attack, shaking and gasping for air as I retreated into my safe place.

So, I turned to even heavier drinking and partying with my friends in a desperate attempt to numb that deep pain—a pain that I later realized only God could heal. I sought refuge, not in the light that heals, but in the artificial neon lights of this old, sinful world. Often we would rent out motel rooms and invite friends over, filling the bathtub with ice to use as our ice chest for our beer and using a five-gallon bucket to make a drink we called "jungle juice." We were drowning our spirits in those buckets of liquor, unaware that the Living Water was still calling my name.

But even though I was still in complete rebellion toward God during this time and for many years after I had run out of that Spirit-filled church, God had never left my side. He was still stretching out to get my attention and was relentlessly reaching his loving arms out toward me. One example of him pursuing me happened when I wanted to have another motel party. I had no money, but I wanted another room to celebrate my birthday. Despite remembering scrambling for money for alcohol, I was completely broke. I went around asking several friends if they knew where I could borrow money, but every avenue I tried was a dead end.

I will never forget what happened next. On my way home from that desperate search, I was taking a road detour and drove through a Kroger parking lot. I was unaware at the time that this physical detour was leading me straight into a divine encounter. I looked down and noticed something on the pavement that looked like a brown leather wallet. My heart skipped a beat as I thought I had just found what I was looking for—it appeared dollar bills were sticking out of the leather! I stopped and ran to pick it up, thinking this was my lucky ticket to fund my birthday bash. But when I picked it up, I quickly realized I had just picked up a Gideon's Bible! The Bible lay flat, and its pages folded upward, mimicking the look of a wallet full of money.

Looking back now, I know God was trying to capture my attention by sending me a sign, saying, "Hey Paula, here is your party! Hey Paula, I can give you a drink from the well that never runs dry," as in John 4:14, "But whosoever drinketh of the water that I shall give him shall never thirst; but the water that I shall give him shall be in him a well of water springing up into everlasting life." God was trying to tell me, "I can heal every place you hurt if you just let me in! Hey Paula, this book is your answer! Alcohol is not your answer! Living in sin is not your answer! I am your answer, Paula!" Yet, I was looking for paper currency, completely blind to the eternal gold I held in my hands. I was too deaf to hear him speaking through this sign. One thing I have learned in my life is, God is always speaking to us, but sometimes we are simply not listening. This was, no doubt, one of those times.

Not long after this, I met a man named Big Tom. We dated shortly after meeting. My mom was certainly not happy about this relationship. I feel it was because she still wanted me with Larry because he was my personal babysitter, and she trusted him. She and Larry had a close relationship. She had never seemed to give Big Tom a chance from the start. I felt Big Tom and I were good together, and he was nothing like Larry. Big Tom was a gentle giant of a man and not toxic at all. He was extremely caring, attentive, and protective of me—but healthily. One thing I desired above anything at this point in my life was to feel protected. I did not fear Big Tom at all, and that brought me the peace and comfort that I had been starving for. Our favorite hangout was Dance Town USA off Airline Drive in Houston, and many weekend nights we would dance, laugh, and drink the night away. This was what I considered therapy for my soul back then.

However, on one of those nights, we partied at Tom's house, drinking and swimming in his indoor pool instead of dancing. I had drunk a little too much again, and Big Tom was afraid to take me home intoxicated. Not knowing my parents very well, he did not want to risk them getting mad at him. So instead, he thought it would be best if we stayed at his house until morning, giving me time to sober up. Well, we ended up pulling into the driveway around five o'clock in the morning, when my daddy was getting ready to leave for work at the crack of dawn. This was a collision course with disaster, just waiting to happen. This was a big mistake.

My parents were extremely upset, and my mother flipped out. She told me I could no longer see Big Tom ever again. Even though I really liked Big Tom, I knew she was serious, and I was not stupid enough to sneak around to see him behind her back. My mama was to be feared, and she did not hand out idle threats. She said what she meant and meant what she said. So, I stopped talking to him without a proper explanation. I felt so bad about this because, truly, Big Tom was good to me. Yet I knew I had to walk away from the gentle giant, and I know it must have broken his heart. But the story did not end there! God, in his divine navigation, had not finished yet with this part of my journey, and I had no way of knowing.

After nearly two decades, he would again permit our paths to cross, offering closure with Tom and a chance to finally acknowledge all Shawn had done for me. I will reveal that divine encounter and what took place in Chapter Eleven.

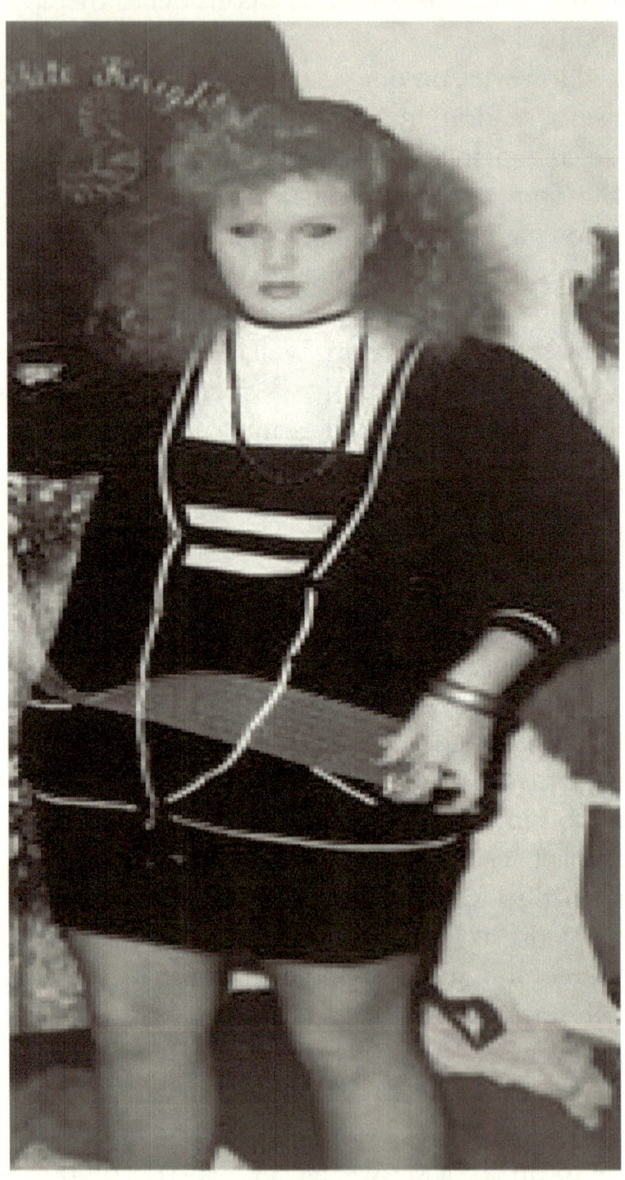

Mama and me

CHAPTER FIVE

THE BADGE AND THE BRIDE

Soon after I broke things off with Larry, my friend Louis introduced me to the man who would later become my husband. I had always felt comfortable hanging around Louis and all his guy friends because I felt like I was part of the group, and I considered them my brothers. They would always look out for me anytime we went anywhere, and I needed that sense of security as I mentioned in the last chapter, so they were a great blessing to me. If a man got out of hand with me in the bars, my brothers were there to take care of business and protect me. The same rules applied to the women if they were to attack them. I still had the anger and fighting in my blood.

Louis and Brad had been friends for several years, but I had never met Brad or seen him at any of the parties, probably because Brad was working his way through the police department's police academy when we met in nineteen ninety-two. But Louis had always tried to play matchmaker and introduced me to different friends of his who were not in the main core of our group. I used to get all excited when he told me he had someone he wanted to introduce me to, and I would spend hours getting all dolled up to meet the person, but it always ended up as a waste of effort. Time after time this would happen, and I would walk away feeling let down by the choice of men he was picking out for his little sister. So, when he told me he wanted me to meet Brad, I put little effort into preparing myself as I had done before. I figured he would end up being just like all the rest. Unknown to me then, this time was going to be far better than the rest.

When I met Brad, I was all giddy like a little schoolgirl, bubbling over with excitement! He was good-looking, extremely smart, courteous, and very polite. He was a chiseled-out police cadet training for a department across the state line in Louisiana. I liked the fact that he was going to be a police officer best of all because in my mind that meant more security and protection. This truly brought me an abundance of peace; feeling this would now be a twenty-four-hours-a-day, seven days a week type of security. We began dating immediately and seemed to get along so well. We would frequent the dance halls together because he loved to dance as well. I also continued the tradition of motel parties with all my crazy friends from school and my new brothers. Now when someone tried calling the police because of our music being loud or something else that disrupted the peace, we could get off the hook. All Brad had to do was tell them he was with the Louisiana agency, flash his badge, and the officers would leave us alone. There were many perks in dating a police officer, and that was just one—and yes, it happened just that easy! I ended up graduating high school in nineteen ninety-three and was so relieved to be getting out of school. I remember how I was beyond ready to celebrate the big occasion of my graduation. The odd thing is that on the day of my actual graduation; I found my mind was not on the fact that I now had a great man in my life or how thrilled I was to be graduating from high school. Instead, my mind was still dwelling on none other than Larry! Literally, as I sat there in my cap and gown waiting for my name to be called, all I could think about was Larry and being so amazed that I was finally free from him! You see, I was still experiencing all the nightmares and random panic attacks, but I was so relieved that I was no longer with him! The depression kept worsening, and the alcohol was no longer working as relief. The person I had been mentally was not who I was anymore.

Toward men, I harbored a deep-seated root of bitterness. Following my experience with Larry and the others, I never fully trusted them. I would use men for what they had to offer, but I never fully trusted them. I made a vow that no man was ever going to hurt me again! I would hurt them before they would have a chance to hurt me. I remember going to counseling and a psychiatrist put me on antidepressants. I was on them for many years. Then they wanted to put me on lithium because they were trying to label me as bipolar, and I declined. It seemed as if nothing the doctor was giving me was helping, though.

Brad proposed to me two years after we first started dating, and although I was happier with him in my life, I was still battling symptoms of Post-Traumatic Stress Disorder. We ended up getting married in the middle of a hot Texas summer of nineteen ninety-four. I was not yet at the legal age to buy alcohol for our wedding, so Brad had to do it. We had a huge, beautiful wedding with lots of food, alcohol, family, and friends. I could not wait to see what was ahead for this new beginning in my life because things were looking brighter as the days continued. Brad was definitely what I felt I needed in my life!

CHAPTER SIX

TRIALS OF AN UNSAVED SOUL

For our honeymoon, Brad and I flew to South Padre Island, and we had a blast! The water there is a lot clearer than our Galveston, Texas, water that we are used to! We rode horses, quadricycle, jet skis, and ate at all the fine local restaurants. Believe it or not, it was also there that I conceived our precious daughter, Alexis. I was so thrilled at the thoughts of having this little bundle of joy in my life. I felt that I would have someone to love me forever; that was a part of me and one I too could love forever! I had been told by my doctor that I might never have a child because of a history of endometriosis. However, a few months prior to the wedding, I had surgery to remove the damaged tissue, and the surgery worked! So, she was our little miracle baby. We were on cloud nine, to say the least! My pregnancy was pretty easy, except for the time I had all four of my wisdom teeth removed five months into the pregnancy. And another time when I was not feeling well again, I ended up passing out on the bathroom floor. When I came to myself, I remember feeling something wet between my legs. I began screaming and crying in fear, thinking it was blood and that I was having a miscarriage—a woman's worst nightmare! Thankfully, it was just urine and not actual blood from a miscarriage after all. I got plenty of rest that week and made a full recovery.

The day came when I went into labor; Brad had planned to play an early game of golf that morning. As he was giving me a goodbye kiss, I told him I was not sure, but I might be in labor. I did not want to mess up his expected golf game, but I could feel the cramping coming on. So, we headed up to the hospital, as directed by my doctor. However, my doctor had previous plans for that day as well, so she ended up breaking my water and then headed out the door for her vacation. Go figure! From that point, I was in labor early in the morning until late afternoon, and when the on-call doctor got stuck in rush hour traffic, the nurse kept telling me not to push. So, by the time I finally received my epidural, there was no time for it to take effect. With three pushes, out came my precious bundle of love.

Alexis weighed in at a whopping nine pounds, eleven ounces, and was twenty-three inches long!

I was so excited that I had this beautiful baby girl! My first words when I saw her were, "I cannot believe I had a baby!" She was the ultimate gift to me. She was so beautiful and looked nothing like me at all, but was a spitting image of her daddy! As soon as I had her, my sister walked out to the waiting room to announce Alexis's arrival. Everyone excitedly asked, "Well, who does she look like?" All my sister could say was, "Just like her daddy." They thought she was teasing until they looked for themselves. She was definitely her daddy's mini-me.

Having a baby around was something new for me because I had never babysat anyone's newborn before. So, when she cried in my hospital room, I did not know what to do for her. I would seriously recommend never having a child until you have spent some time babysitting one! The nurse so graciously came into the room and showed me how to change her diaper and gave me some simple instructions on what to check when she cried. So, I used the list the nurse provided, and it worked well until the hospital discharged me and I had to manage alone. Then nothing I tried worked, not even the nurse's checklist. My beautiful bundle of love began crying nonstop! I took her to the doctor and was told she had an ear infection. He gave her some antibiotics, and that helped for a while, but the infection returned. I went back and forth to the doctor with back-to-back ear infections.

She would cry for hours at a time, so I could not get much sleep, and my nerves were getting worse as the weeks passed by. Even when her ear infections calmed down, she screamed at the top of her lungs. I detested my inability to help my precious baby and my lack of knowledge regarding her condition. I would utilize all the tricks from the nurse's list and any additional ones I acquired. I knew she did not have an ear infection, but I could see she was in pain. I took her to the doctor again and told him he had to help me because something was wrong with my baby. That was when he diagnosed her with colic and prescribed Myla icon drops for her. But though I gave her the drops as the doctor directed, they still did not work on her. This child continued to scream all night long. She would clutch her fists together, turn red as a hot chili pepper, and just let the screams roll hour after hour while I frantically did everything, I knew to try to help her. I even had two very close friends that I considered family come to help me when they could. Both Puddin and Mandy were sisters, and they were always so good at trying to help soothe her.

In the daytime, I was walking around like a zombie and felt as if I was losing my mind. I began to battle severe postpartum depression. And although my emotions were crashing all over the place, I kept trying to find relief for her. I tried different methods, like taking her out on the swing in the front yard at two and three o'clock in the morning, hoping to calm her down. It did not work. I would slowly and gently rock her in my rocking chair, thinking that might help. I would try rocking her faster and singing nursery rhymes to her. I would get up at four o'clock in the morning and take her for drives around town as we listened to music in the car. I would put her in her carrier on top of the washing machine on the spin cycle. I was told to leave a vacuum cleaner running, and the sound would help her calm down. Believe it or not, the vacuum cleaner actually worked, and that was the only thing that seemed to work! Yet, after a few hours of running it, I was afraid of it catching fire. As soon as I hit the off button, she would start wailing and screaming all over again from the top of her little lungs! I tried everything I could to calm her down, while I was getting worse mentally and felt like I was becoming psychotic all over again! Mind you, I still had not fully recovered from my mental issues from the previous part of my journey with Larry and the others. I was still battling all the symptoms of Post-Traumatic Stress Disorder and suffering with the nightmares. I was suffering from postpartum depression and trying to deal with my screaming newborn. The spiritual warfare I was battling just kept getting thicker!

I remember thinking that I was no longer the same person I used to be at all. I felt I had lost who I was as an individual and my mind was too far gone. I would cry and cry, wondering if I could ever think normally again. My mind was chaotic, and I was in a deep dark pit being tormented twenty-four-seven! I had no peace or mental clarity at all! When the doctor suggested lithium, I was originally too scared to take it due to all the side effects. However, at this point, I was becoming desperate for a resolution to all the madness inside my head and was now pondering the lithium idea. I also was considering doing what a cousin had done, and that was electric shock therapy. This is where they place leads on your head and force electricity through the bone of the skull to help heal a person from depression. In this process, they give the person a rubber bite block placed between their teeth as a barrier. This is to help absorb the bone-crushing force of the jaw clenching, shielding the tongue from being severed and the teeth from shattering when the electrical currents hit the individual's skull. I knew it was a brutal remedy, and I also knew the consequences of shock therapy treatment. I realized I might end up with no memory at all. I considered if the potential loss of memory of my husband or daughter from treatments was a worthwhile risk for achieving a mind without depression.

So, having to deal with a sick, crying baby around the clock added fuel to the raging fire in my mind. I rarely slept, and my frayed nerves really got to me! I was in desperate need and had no clue what was wrong with me mentally or with my child physically. Her crying lasted for a solid year. I never shook my baby during those episodes like we hear of so many parents doing. However, because of the nonstop crying, I began to understand how those people could have snapped under such intense mental pressures—especially those who did not have God in their lives. I learned the hard way to have empathy for those mothers who were battling postpartum depression and the pressures of raising young children.

Especially when they are sick around the clock. I ended up getting a job hoping it might give me some temporary mental relief from full-time motherhood. I felt like a horrible mother for leaving her as I went to work, but I was unsure of what else to do. However, this decision paid off well in the long term, as you shall see in the next chapter. It was a divine encounter of the God kind! Oh, the love of our great God! His mercy is never ending. Through the Lord's mercies we are not consumed, because his compassions fail not. They are new every morning; great is your faithfulness (Lamentations 3:22–23).

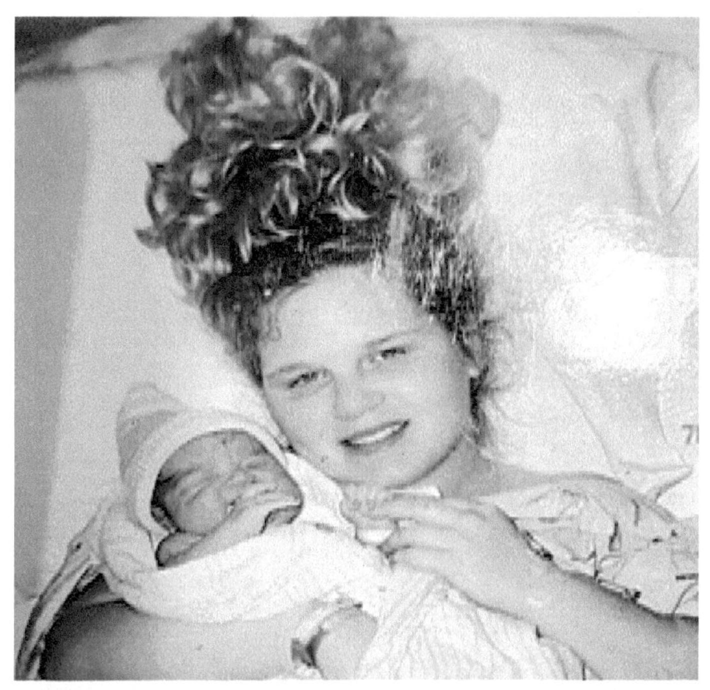

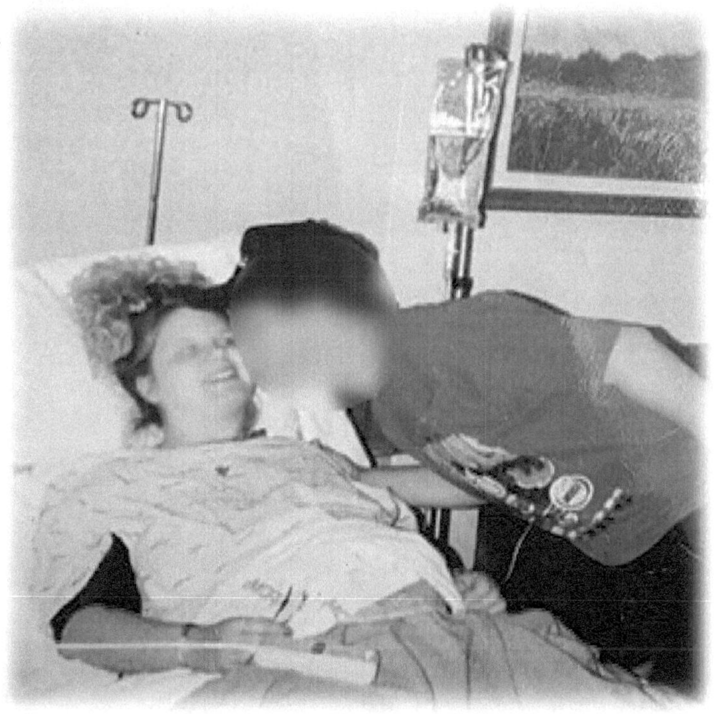

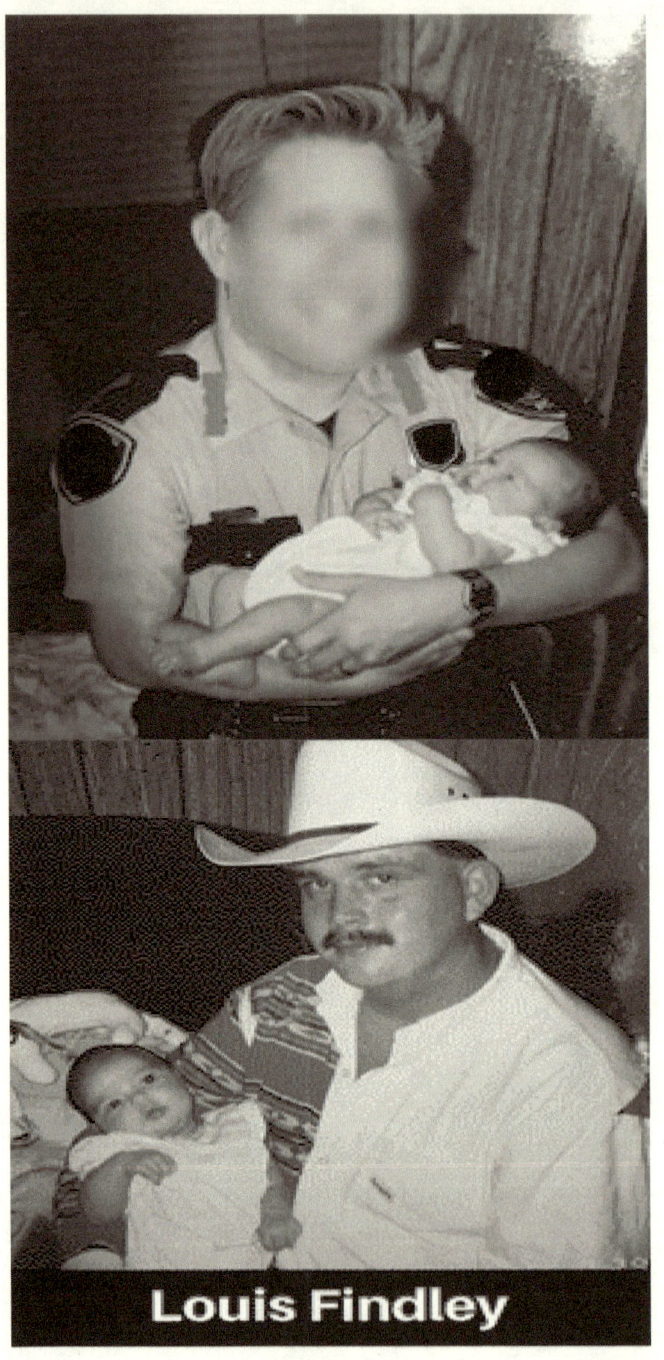

Louis Findley

CHAPTER SEVEN

THE COST OF SIN

At my new job, I quickly got acquainted with a coworker named Terrie, who invited me to church one evening in nineteen ninety-six. She was also married to a police officer and had three small children, my daughter's age. So, we had a lot in common, and as a young mother, I needed a friend whom I had things in common with. I was not interested in going to church, per se, but I needed the friendship she offered, and she was always a ball of fun to hang out with. I was not really expecting anything to happen that night, but God had other plans. She took me to Lakewood Church, The Oasis of Love. I remember Pastor John Osteen preaching a fiery message that night, but I am not sure to this day what his message was even on. All I know is the convicting power of God hit me like a pop fly ball coming right out to left field, hitting me right between my eyes!

I wept under the convicting power and presence of an almighty God! My tears flowed like a turbulent fountain as I repented before the Lord. My biggest sin and greatest regret that haunted me so frequently was the abortion, so I yielded to the overwhelming burden to repent and ask God to forgive me. The guilt had eaten at me like cancer for so many years. I remember feeling so bad that night for what I had done, and I just wanted forgiveness! But even though I was repenting, I had no confidence in my heart that God would forgive someone as bad as me.

I recall him asking everyone to come to the front of the church, so I complied. Too ashamed to look up, I stood before Pastor John Osteen with my head hung low, my gaze fixed on the floor. I could not even open my mouth to utter a word aloud. All I could do was cry and tell Jesus how sorry I was. I felt so bad for doing what I had done so many years prior. That was when Pastor Osteen got my attention by saying to me, "Hey, look up here!" When I looked up at this mighty man of God, he looked straight into my eyes and said, "It is okay. God has forgiven you! God has forgiven you! You can rejoice now!" I tried to take his word for it and rejoice, but I was so consumed with the burden of my sin, I did not know how to forgive myself.

However, the next day I felt different and good inside. I was not out of the weeds mentally, but I knew I felt some kind of change had taken place the night before. I had no clue that my walk with God was something I needed to keep up with and cultivate. I was still dealing with my crying child at home and the demons of depression. My church attendance wasn't regular, but I visited occasionally. Let me clearly share with you that God wants full custody of his children and not just weekend visits. The devil is not a part-time devil, so why would we want to be part-time Christians? However, I did not know that at this time.

At least one year had passed after this encounter with God at Lakewood Church, and then God gave me my very first dream as an adult. In this dream, I saw a baby rolling around in my stomach. I could see the outline of the baby, and the dream was extremely clear. I woke up frightened by how real it had felt. By this time, I had left that job where I had met Terrie and was already working at an insurance company and taking evening college courses to earn my certification in Human Resource Management. And it was in one of those classes that I met Vickie, whom God would use next in my life.

Vickie came up to me one night and introduced herself. When we began making small talk for a while, for some odd reason she came right out and asked if I had a church home where I regularly attended church. I told her, "Yes, as a matter of fact, I do." (That was a lie because I was not attending faithfully.) She asked me which one, and I told her Lakewood Church. Of course, I acted as if I were a dedicated member because I did not want to look bad in front of her. She then asked me if I was going to the upcoming event they were putting on. At that point, I am sure she could sense that I was not the faithful member that I was trying to portray myself to be because I was clearly dumbfounded and lost for words!

Instead, I looked like a deer caught in headlights when I realized she knew about this church too and was probably an active member. I started stumbling over my words and quickly changed the topic. I felt like the kid who had just gotten her hand caught in the cookie jar! Talk about getting busted! I had not yet fully surrendered to God!

A week went by, and she came up to me and said, "God wanted me to tell you that you are fixing to go through a trial but not to worry, that everything will be okay." Well, I did not give her or the words she had spoken much thought at all. Instead, I chalked it up in my mind that Vickie was off her rocker for saying God had spoken to her. I thought she was some crazy Christian! I still was clueless that God could actually speak to people, especially since she was just a student in my class and not a preacher.

I also remember during this time a friend had given me some marital advice saying, "When you get bored in your marriage bed, just pretend you are having intercourse with someone else besides your husband." Obviously, that was not biblical advice from a Godly woman, mind you. But a few nights later, I found myself following her advice and imagining I was having intercourse with my boss. Then, after a couple of weeks had passed, I realized I was late on my monthly cycle. My fears were confirmed when I took a pregnancy test. It was positive!

When I realized I was pregnant again, fear immediately got a death grip on me! I could not bear the thought of enduring the mental torture of another screaming child, sleepless nights, and more postpartum depression, feeling as if I was losing my mind all over again! I had no clue how to survive another round of this life cycle mentally! In the meantime, I was still playing games with God, never fully dedicating myself to him or his house! I would often go to the nightclub on Saturday and occasionally end up at church on Sunday. God was not the Lord of my life. I was the lord over my life and added God in whenever I wanted to.

Due to me playing games with God, I was open prey for satan, and unknown to me then, he had all legal rights to take me out! If we do not surrender fully to the Lord Jesus Christ, He is not bound to His Word to protect us. God is a God of covenant. A covenant binds two mutual parties who dedicate themselves to working together. I was not working with God or making him the Lord over my life. I was living for one person, and that was my own stinking flesh.

Because of the fear of being pregnant again and not knowing how to mentally deal with it all again, satan put it in my heart to kill my innocent child. And the words of Mrs. Vickie, the woman I thought was so crazy from college, began to haunt me, echoing in my ears. I knew this was the trial she had warned me about.

When I went to have the abortion, I said a quick prayer asking God, "If you do not want me to go through with this abortion, please somehow put a stop to it." He would have said, "We can do this together. You do not need to have an abortion. You have what it takes to get through this, and I will help you." I genuinely believe that if that had been the case, I would never have gone to the appointment in the first place. However, he was nonchalant, unsaved, and said it was my choice that he stood by me regardless of my decision. He did not really care either way, and he told me that.

The doctor came in to do his exam before the procedure and told me it was too early to have the abortion and to come back in a couple of weeks. You would have thought that I would have been excited because I had just received the answer to my prayer! You would have thought that by the doctor saying those words to me, I would have kept my child because God had stopped it, just as I had asked.

However, that is not the way this story ended. Instead, that was when a different type of extreme spiritual warfare of the mind came hard and heavy at me! That is when I entered another mental torture chamber of hell.

At the time, I didn't realize there were varying degrees of demonic torment that I was undergoing due to granting the demons complete access to myself. I made the decision not to live for God by listening to the enemy! I was the one who chose to walk in sin and to have an abortion. So, as a result, they had open access to take me deeper into the demonic torture. I was on a ride from the pits of hell itself and had no clue how to get off! I began losing my mind, far worse than before. My mind, which was never strong, was now not just weak, but also taken over and hijacked by demonic influences. The enemy tortured me by reminding me of the night I pretended to be having intercourse with another man. He tormented my thoughts and told me the child was not even my husband's but the other man's. I felt so guilty for imagining having intercourse with my boss. The enemy loved using this guilt against my mind, on top of all the rest of my fears. I was so paranoid and depressed; it was horrific! All the while, I would hear Mrs. Vickie's words in my head, booming in my ears, extremely loud.

I became extremely paranoid, to the point of looking for Mrs. Vickie everywhere I went, thinking she was following me. At traffic lights, I would look over to see if she was sitting in the car next to us. I would look for her behind bushes or between shelves in the stores we went into. Anywhere and everywhere, I was looking for this woman to pop up like a Jack-in-the-box. Demons tormented my mind while I was counting the days until I could run to the abortion clinic to get the abortion over with. I thought if I just got it over with, I would escape the mental torment. They were literally screaming demons in my ears and making me feel as if I was losing my mind. I kept hearing Mrs. Vickie's words echoing loudly, nonstop, and very intrusively.

Finally, the day came for me to have the abortion, and I went through with killing yet another one of my children. I will never forget what I felt when my eyes opened after the anesthesia wore off in that recovery room. There were literally no thicker, dark, demonic clouds that had been following me day and night, tormenting me since the day I discovered I was pregnant! The demonic presence was gone. There were no more tormenting demons, nor extreme paranoia, and no Mrs. Vickie's voice echoing in my head loudly. There were no more accusations that the child was not my husband's screaming at me. My mind went back to the way it had been before all this happened. The voices were gone, and I was back in a decent state of mind.

But at that point, the realization of what I had just done hit me like a ton of bricks. I began to yell and scream in the middle of the recovery room, placing my hands on my stomach, crying loudly, repeating over and over, "Oh dear God, I am so sorry! Oh, dear God, I am so sorry!!! You can give me a miracle. You can put my baby back in my stomach. Please help me, God! Please put my baby back in my stomach, God! I did not mean to do this! Please HELP ME Lord! Forgive me, Jesus, for killing my baby! Help me!" The nurses were scrambling around in a frenzy, not knowing how to handle the crisis, because I was causing such a ruckus in the recovery room. I remember being so loud and just crying, begging God to put my baby back inside me. My thinking was clear; there was no more fog of darkness, and I knew what I had done! The nurses quickly removed me from the recovery room because there were other women waking up from their own anesthesia and hearing everything I was screaming. I am sure they thought they had a madwoman on their hands, and she was not good for their baby-killing business.

I did not know then, but I know now that a demon was sent on a special assignment to hijack my mind and torment me until I killed my child, God's creation! I had given him legal access to do so, too, by yielding to his voice and the intrusive thoughts. The devil would not allow me to have absolutely no peace until I fulfilled his demonic desire! You talk about adding another bomb of destruction to my life!

However, that was the pivotal point in history for me! The Bible says in Genesis 50:20, "But as for you, ye thought evil against me: but God meant it unto good, to bring to pass, as it is this day, to save many people alive." God took the harm the devil meant for me and turned it for my good. After that devastating experience, I hit those church doors, and I meant business this time! I went to the altar again and repented once more for killing yet another child! It was difficult, but I placed one foot in front of the other and kept walking. I began to go on a regular basis back to Lakewood Church with Pastor John Osteen. While still battling depression, I considered shock therapy as a means of relief. Spiritual warfare was completely unknown to me, and I did not know I could combat it through God. I was also clueless about how to really serve God, even though I was trying my best. I was showing up to church and attending alone because my husband did not want to go with me. Yet I still felt like I was lacking some pieces to this spiritual puzzle.

I started noticing something different about going to church this time around, though. I noticed that every time I would boldly step out of my comfort zone and go up for prayer, things slowly began to change for me.

There was always this one sweet, blonde, slender lady who would wear the most pleasant smile on her face as she stood at the front of the church, waiting to pray for those who needed prayer. I always gravitated toward her and requested that she pray with me. Her name was Elaine Perez. While she was praying for me, I felt normal and in my right mind for those few moments. But when she stopped, I would start feeling what I would call crazy in the mind again, as I would return to my seat. Then when they started the praise and worship, I would again feel halfway normal and in my right mind again, at least during that part of the service. But when the praise and worship stopped, the crazy feeling in my mind would start back up. This cycle kept going for a while. However, I noticed the more I went to church and went up for Elaine to pray for me, the longer the peace and normal feeling lasted. And that same calmness I felt during the church service began lasting longer and longer each week. Finally, it got to where I could leave the church parking lot and remain in what I would call my right mind for about fifteen minutes—then a few weeks later it would increase to thirty minutes, then an hour, then two hours, etc. Slowly but surely, and unknown to me then, I was getting delivered from the demons of depression that had wreaked so much havoc in my daily life! I was getting free from the demons that controlled me every single day for years! These were the same demons that drove me to drink, to hurt others, sleep around, to steal, kill, to cut myself, and attempt suicide, all because I did not understand the spiritual realm. I learned during this season that God had the answer for all the spiritual warfare I was experiencing, that the doctors wanted to label as my mental illness. I learned the Lord was bigger than what the enemy had inflicted on me for all those many years. Generational curses, as described in the

Bible, along with the open doors of abuse, were major sources of the depression I had struggled with.

Generational curses pass down from one generation to the next and can appear in many forms. A generational curse is a curse that is passed down because someone in the family chose sin over obeying God's Word. You can read about this in Exodus 20:5. The Bible says that the iniquity of the fathers is passed down to the children to the third and fourth generation. The medical field likes to label such issues when they see them as a family disease or something hereditary. This can include mental illnesses, physical illnesses, relationship troubles, and even financial issues. This can also include constant run-ins with the law and going to jail. When you see a family having several people battling the same type of battles—such as heart disease, diabetes, constant lack, bitterness, divorce, lust, drug addiction, pornography addiction, alcoholism, sexual abuse, poverty, mental illnesses, witchcraft, breaking the law, etc.—that is usually a good sign you are dealing with a generational curse and need to break it off your family's bloodline through the power of God and prayer. You need to repent sincerely to God, on behalf of yourself and your ancestors, for what you feel has been the generational curse. Verbally denounce the works of darkness and all ungodly soul ties with authority. Renounce every unholy covenant that has previously been made.

Forgive your ancestors and yourself. Declare that you will have no part in this evil any longer and that Jesus Christ has made you free and stand on God's Word! "If the Son therefore shall make you free, ye shall be free indeed." John 8:36. Now seal it by applying the precious blood of Jesus Christ over you and your entire family. Live a godly lifestyle and choose daily to surrender to God.

ELAINE PEREZ

Terrie and me

Mama Dodie

Therefore if any man be in Christ, he is a new creature: old things are passed away; behold, all things are become new. 2 Corinthians 5:17

CHAPTER EIGHT

UNMASKING THE SHAME

I was so thrilled to be free from the demons of depression and oppression and finally felt like I was on a winning streak as I grew closer and closer to God.

Internally, I had this overwhelming desire to get water baptized! On one particular night that I felt this stirring in my spirit, I was at my friend Susie's house, and she was dyeing my hair. I heard her mom mention she was going to church at Lakewood that night, too. I was so excited because I knew this was a setup from God. The Holy Spirit was drawing me so heavily to get water baptized, and I had already planned on going that night, but I really did not want to go alone. It started getting late, and as my hair was still in the middle of processing, I started seeing a purple tint in the strands of hair. I knew it was time to leave for church, but satan started putting thoughts in my head to not go, telling me I would have purple hair and look funny. However, I felt so strongly in my heart that I should go that I did not care if I went to church with purple or wet hair. I was determined that nothing would stop me from getting baptized that night! Thank God, my hair did not come out purple, but I ended up running out the door with a wet head.

Now, for some of you, that might not be that big of a deal. However, for me, it was huge! I went nowhere with wet hair and still do not to this day. I am so thankful, though, for the deep burning in my soul that night to get baptized, no matter the cost to my flesh. I recall that when I got there; I saw lots of family members in attendance watching their loved ones, celebrating the special occasion, and taking pictures. I did not know people celebrated these events because I was not raised in church. I knew little if anything at this point. All I knew was that I was supposed to get water baptized. I had no family or friends there with me besides Susie's mother—and certainly no pictures or videos to remember the special occasion.

However, I kept pressing on in this spiritual journey with no one going to church with me. My aunt, who is the Pastor lives in another state from me, or I would have gone with her. Often, I would get invited to the singles group because everyone thought I was single, since my husband never went with me. I also would attend Billie Hunt's women's Bible study in The Woodlands. And I was learning from various great men and women of God, especially Joyce Meyer. Her book, Beauty for Ashes, really helped me. I was learning so much about healing and deliverance from wrong mindsets—especially my own! With all the abuse I had endured, there came a day when God said it was time to deal with some false mindsets I had taken on. One was how I viewed sexual intercourse—I thought it was disgusting, and it made me feel dirty. I would never withhold from my husband sexually, but I never had peace or felt right about having intercourse, ever. It was literally a cold and heartless act that I performed to please my mate, and that was it.

My biggest learning curve and deliverance in this area did not happen in a church service by someone laying hands on me. It came not from a book I read, a sermon I watched, a counseling session, or even some great big deliverance service.

Instead, it happened in my own private bed, as my husband and I were engaged in full-blown intimacy. My bed literally turned into the classroom, believe it or not! God was determined to deliver me from my erroneous mindset about sex. Let me add in here that yes, God wants you to enjoy sexual intercourse! And if that is shocking for you to hear and for your mind to grasp, then you, too, probably need to be set free in this area, as I needed it. Sexual intercourse is a beautiful thing between a husband and a wife, but I never knew this, and I know there are many of you who do not know this either. These mindsets cause major issues in the marriage bed, and couples avoid discussing them (especially the partner who has experienced sexual abuse, regardless of whether it is the husband or wife). But please be mindful of the fact that I said marriage beds! Sexual intercourse is only reserved for those who are married and not dating. Otherwise, you are in sin and committing acts that are against God's will. God intended sex for married couples, and he created it for both enjoyment and to multiply the human race.

Now back to this deliverance from the wrong mindset: as my husband and I were having intercourse, God began speaking to me right dab in the middle of the act. I was like, "Umm, God, we are having intercourse right now; cannot this wait until church time?" God was not about waiting at all. He was about delivering me in his timeline, not mine—and in his way, not Paula's way! God began telling me how I had been viewing sexual intercourse as something dirty, telling me my mindset had been wrong for many years. He told me I needed to relax and not be fearful because this was something he had created for a husband and wife to enjoy together. I had tears rolling down my face as God was dealing with me and delivering me from the wrong thoughts and feelings I had held all those years. My husband never even noticed. He had no clue about the spiritual battle that was going on in that bed and in my head at that moment. I would try to relax as God instructed me to do, and then I would tense back up. I would try to relax and then tense back up. On that bed, I was literally crying out to God, begging for His help to release me from these terrible feelings of shame. This mental warfare went back and forth for a while, but finally, I was set free. I was forever changed, and my viewpoint of sex was no longer something deemed as dirty or unclean. It was now something beautiful and holy between my husband and me.

That might sound odd, the way God delivered me, but God does not have cookie-cutter patterns for how he delivers each of his children. The way he delivered me might not be the same way he delivers you. We cannot put God in a box; we must allow him to move the way he wants to move and obey.

So yes, I was growing in many areas as God introduced me to different ministers. Not long after that,

I joined Lakewood Church's volunteer ministry. I worked at the information booth and met a lot of amazing people. One great couple I became friends with was Reggie and Sheila Warren. I then volunteered during the day for the Lakewood Church office, assisting a precious sister named Kathy Osborn, Lisa Comes' secretary. I was really growing in God and having an amazing time learning about the Lord.

One day, Kathy told me that the office manager was seeking someone to fill the church receptionist position and asked if I would be interested in it. I was so excited and overjoyed by the news, thinking, who would not want that position? A funny thing happened, though. When Kathy asked me about taking the position, she also suggested that I pray about it before responding. I knew this woman walked with God and had a lot of wisdom, but at that time, I thought she was crazy for suggesting I pray about it. The next time I saw her, I asked her a few more questions concerning the duties that would be expected of me and was told that part of the duties included taking an overflow of phone calls. With those phone calls, there would be times I might need to pray with people. Now that made me second-guess taking the position, because the thought of having to pray for someone over the phone petrified me at that time. Even amidst all that, I still wanted the position deep down inside. To me, it was the cream of the crop, and I could not ask for anything better! I figured God would find a way to help me get through praying for someone. Yet with Kathy's words and wisdom, I yielded to what she suggested, and I was still praying about it.

Then one night, God gave me a dream where Dodie Osteen and I were standing side by side at their beautiful reception desk talking. But in this dream, I felt so inadequate and out of place as I stood there talking to

Mrs. Dodie. You see, in the dream, I did not have any shoes on. Though young in my faith and uncertain about dream interpretation, I knew God was trying to tell me something. I knew I had my answer and that somehow God was telling me not to take the position. I was heartbroken and did not understand why God would tell me to decline the offer, but I went back to the church and told Kathy and the other ladies that God said I could not take the position. The other ladies were shocked and asked me why not? I told them I did not know that answer. I just knew God was telling me no.

Kathy seemed to understand, though. It was as if God had shown her already or something. I was still green behind the ears about the spiritual things of God, as some country people would say. But I am so thankful for Kathy guiding me at that time and on several other occasions during that time of my life.

When we volunteered for the office, we were always asked to stay in the copy room area with the rest of the volunteers to do our work, not to roam down the hallways. There were good and valid reasons for this request because down the hallway was where all the ministry offices were located. I always got along well with everyone there and chatted with different staff members and ministers. In fact, that was where I first met precious Reverend Sam Martin—the one who won Pastor John Osteen to the Lord. He often asked me to come help him with various projects he was working on. But this was where Kathy had to shed some light for me. She took me aside one day and explained to me what the word favor meant. She explained God had given me much favor in my life—more so than some of the other volunteers. So, she asked if I could try to remain in the work area with the other volunteers because it was only fair. She had such a wonderful way of explaining things to me. I loved working with her and learning from her. She was also another very powerful prayer warrior at Lakewood.

Later, Reverend Sam Martin began working in his home satellite office, and I went there to help him instead of at the church. He had a precious wife also named Paula, whom I would also help by taking her to her beauty shop appointments and doing random things. Sam became one of my greatest mentors and a lifelong friend. I counted it a privilege every time I had the chance to glean from this man's great wisdom and any opportunity to spend time with him. Reverend Sam Martin was so different from anyone I have ever met in my entire life, even until this very day. He never held normal conversations like regular people. When he spoke, it was solely the Bible that came out of his mouth. He fought a lot of physical attacks against his body, and I knew he would be in pain often. When I would ask him how he felt that day, he would never answer the question as I expected; he would quote a Bible verse about healing. If I were to ask him about the weather, he would come up with a Bible scripture about the weather. He literally was a walking Bible and kept a guard over his mouth like I had never seen before. On one occasion, when I was taking him to his dialysis appointment, he shared with me how he won souls for Jesus. He would tell people he had crossed paths with that he had a best friend and brag about all the wonderful things his best friend had done for him throughout his entire lifetime. Then, after building his friend up so high, he would tell them his friend's name was Jesus and share with them they could be best friends with Jesus, too. When he was in the hospital and was fixing to cross over into Glory, my daughter, Cammy, sang for him. I will never forget watching his spirit man react to her singing "Amazing Grace." He could not speak, but he fully responded to the spirit of God and the anointing that was on that song. It was as if his spirit man was lifting his body off that hospital bed, as he was trying to drink from the holy waters of Heaven. I was as close to Brother Sam as I was to my own grandpa. He was such a humble man who cared so much for souls. He was always on the hunt to win a soul for Jesus! I learned a lot from those early days at Lakewood Church and was thankful for it.

It was not long after Pastor John's passing over into Glory in January nineteen ninety-nine, and after Reverend Sam Martin's passing, when God moved me. This is also when God revealed the meaning of the dream I had while I was at Lakewood Church. God gave me Ephesians 6:12, where it talks about the armor of God and how our feet needed to be shod with the preparation of the Gospel.

Then I understood the image of me not wearing shoes as I was talking to Mama Dodie that day. God knew I did not have enough of his Word in me to sustain me for the position. He knew that I still had some training I needed to go through.

The process of how God moved me to my new church was amazing, though. At the time I was attending Lakewood, I was also attending County Line Cowboy Church with Pastor Ted Woods and visiting Pastor Ben Priest's church, River of God. Pastor Ted and I worked as a team in the early start of his church. The services were being held in the auction area of a feed store in Magnolia. I was still growing, and so was Pastor Ted, and it was at his church that I preached my first sermon. I will never forget getting up that morning with a fiery word from God in my spirit.

But that day, a gentleman who had been going to that church for a while had really tested me. He was probably in his late fifties, weighing about three hundred pounds, and he had lain flat across the stadium-style seating. It was very noticeable for everyone there; you could see them looking at him in bewilderment. I felt he had done this on purpose, acting as if the message was so boring he went to sleep, as an attack against me for being a woman preacher. His behavior took me aback, yet I tried to keep it from affecting my sermon. God spoke to me and told me, "Do not pay any attention to him; you just focus on me! You preach my word!" So, I kept preaching as God instructed me to do. Then, after the service, one of this man's friends approached me and rebuked me for being a woman preacher. So, I got hammered really good that day with a double whammy. The enemy did not like the fact that I had stepped out in faith and had followed my calling as a preacher that morning. I did not care, though, and I kept on trucking with Jesus. God was moving in my life, and it was very clear.

During this time, my Aunt Myrtle, who was a pastor in Turkey Oak, Missouri, visited us. She asked if I wanted to attend a camp meeting service with her at the family church on Saturday night. This was the same church I had run out of when I was a teen, full of the devil. I had remained scared of what had happened there for so many years, and I was afraid to go, but I thought, what do I have to lose? I was an adult and decided not to fear that place any longer. So, I agreed to go with her. That night, the power of God fell in that church like I had never seen before, and I experienced a new level of the Spirit of God that lasted throughout the night.

When I woke up Sunday morning, I was still physically shaking from the power of God that I had experienced the previous night, and in fact, it lingered on me for at least one week or more! So much so that when I went back to the County Line Cowboy Church, a lady came up requesting prayer for a toothache. I laid my hands on her cheek, closed my eyes, and prayed for her tooth. When I was done, I said amen and opened my eyes. But the lady was no longer standing before me. I was shocked, and I did not understand what had just happened! I looked down, and there she was, lying on the floor of that old feed store. She had fallen out under the power of God. Some church members did not like what had just happened and were just as shocked. They had never seen God move like that in this church before, and they were not ready for it. Although Pastor Ted and I had experienced it ourselves, we had not seen it happen there yet. It reminded me of the time that R.W. Schambach visited Lakewood Church and laid hands on me. I, too, was not expecting to fall out when the power of God hit me like a ton of bricks and the lights went out.

So, it was clear the power of God was in that little family church that I had run out of years before. A few days after that incident, God spoke to me and told me I needed to stop attending the River of God Church. I did not understand why. My thought was that God had instructed Pastor Ted to launch Wednesday night church services, and my role would be to help him on those evenings. I just knew God did not want me to stop attending church on Wednesday nights, but I was unsure of what he was trying to say to me. So, I called Pastor Ted and asked him if God had told him to have Wednesday night church services. He said, "No, ma'am." I said, "But are you SURE?" He said, "Yes, I am sure!"

So, when I prayed, asking God to show me what he wanted me to do, suddenly, that old country church popped into my head. "Oh, no God!" I exclaimed." I loved that church service, and I had a marvelous time, but not that church! I recall assuring Him that I'd attend any church he chose, except for that particular one. That root of fear from when I was a teenager running out of those church doors still lingered. That devil wanted to make sure I continued to fear that church for a long time. But then I felt the Spirit of God go silent. He had stopped speaking to me, and I felt his presence leave me. So, I put a fleece out before God. I said, "Okay God, if you want me to go to that church, I want the pastor himself to call me up on the phone and invite me personally." I waited all day long for the phone to ring, and nothing happened. I got excited and thought, thank you, Jesus, I do not have to go back to that church! However, three days later, the pastor himself, Reverend Gene Doyle, called me on the phone and invited me back to the church. I was blown away because God had answered my fleece, and the pastor called me on the phone. I always laugh at God's sense of humor for having me wait for those three days, though. God works on his timeline and not ours. That is when I became a member of Houston Revival Temple Church.

God's Generals
Lakewood Chuch

CHAPTER NINE

WAR AGAINST THE WITCH

Now that the enemy saw me taking on new spiritual territory at Houston Revival Temple Church with Pastors Gene and Lorine Doyle, he did not like it. I had truly become a threat to the kingdom of darkness. During this time, I was serving as a youth leader at the church, and the teenagers were truly being touched by God. Their lives were changing and being set free; it was so beautiful to witness their transformations. I was also drawing closer in intimacy with God through my devotion time. I would lock myself away in my prayer room to read and pray for hours at a time. Most days I would spend between five and seven hours with God, one-on-one. There were a few times I experienced where the power of God would be so strong in that prayer room that when I walked in, it was hard for me to even remain standing on my feet because of the lingering presence of the Lord. There were several occasions I would walk through Walmart or at a restaurant eating, and I would hear the voice of God so easily from the hours of devotion with him.

God would then give me special words to deliver to the surrounding people to encourage them with hope. I marveled at how clearly I was hearing the voice of God, and it was precious to me. It felt like I was walking in a Holy Ghost glory cloud or in the Garden of Eden before the fall of Adam and Eve. The enemy was mad at this new level of intimacy and the new territory I had been gaining spiritually. That is when he began his plot to try to take me out through another attack of mental warfare. During these years, I learned that the enemy of our soul loves to study our lives. He knows all of our weak spots and our strengths. In fact, he is the one who helps create our weak spots by orchestrating painful and hurtful events to take place early on. This is what many call a grooming process. He will groom us so he can use those past hurts to set us up for sabotage later. The enemy knew he could not get me to fall into my past sinful lifestyle, as he had done so easily before. Yet, he still knew he needed a door of legal access to attack in attempts to stop me from fulfilling my calling and destiny. The enemy cannot just trespass into a child of God's life to remain there without us giving him legal access first. So, what did he do to gain legal access? He went for the next closest thing to me—my husband—my weak spot. If the enemy cannot get to us, he will always try to attack those closest to us. My husband remained unsaved, despite my praying for his salvation for several years.

One big reason I had even agreed to marry him in the first place is that I felt safe with him around other women. That was a huge deal for me to have confidence that he would not cheat on me. The enemy is a calculated strategist though. He knew that after years of being groomed by past betrayals, cheating was the one weapon I had no defense against. It was a blow below the belt, specifically designed to shatter me because he knew I would not handle it well. The enemy also knew that I had always vowed that I would never put up with another cheater. I would have never guessed in a million years though that he would have cheated on me, but I began noticing some troublesome changes in his behavior. My husband was not the type to have friends or go anywhere on his own. He went to work and came home as a dedicated husband, but that suddenly changed. And the more I prayed, the worse it got. He began hanging out with other police officers from work, which was not his norm, and started doing other things that were just out of character for him. I also recall him starting to venture out and attend hard rock concerts, as I stayed home with our daughter. I noticed he switched from his years of wearing plain white Fruit of the Loom underwear to stylish boxers out of nowhere. For the first time in his life, he got colored contacts that changed his deep brown eyes to blue. I remember attending a BBQ at the home of my best friend from high school, and when my husband walked off, they turned to me and said, "You need to keep your eyes on Brad." I was like, "What?" This friend had never said such a thing before, yet they could pick up that something was off with my husband as well. When the police department invited us to the substation for an employee fish fry, I finally noticed something was really off. My husband and the other officers acted differently around me. I could not put my finger on what exactly was going on, but I knew something was smelling fishy, and it was not the fish at the fish fry either!

My husband and I hardly ever fought. I can only remember one real argument that we had in our marriage, and that was because I had painted a wooden beam in the house that he asked me not to paint. That was the only time we ever had an actual fight. But when he came home one night and, out of nowhere, started an argument with me; I knew something was wrong. He then told me, with a sigh of exasperation, that he was sick of my praying for everyone who called our home seeking prayer. He was sick of seeing me read my Bible. He was sick of me going to church all the time. The old Paula he had married was what he wanted back, he said, as I was no longer the same. He told me he wanted me to start going back to the bars with him again, and if not, he said he was divorcing me.

At this stage in my life, I had been learning about submission. For many years I said I would never submit myself to a man because when you do, they just hurt you in the end. I would not give a man power over my life ever again. So, God had been working really hard on delivering me from this wrong mindset and pack of lies the enemy had sold me on the topic of submission. So, in my desire to please God, I told my husband that I would stop all those things that he requested of me. I thought by agreeing to my husband's demands this was pleasing to God because after all, this was submission. I knew deep down though I was not going to any bars with him, but I figured I would cross that bridge later when I got there. As soon as those words left my lips and I verbally agreed with him to stop all the things he wanted me to stop, I literally felt something inside me just sink. It was such a strong sinking feeling of sadness lodged in the pit of my stomach. I did not understand it or know what I was feeling, but I knew something was not right.

That was the first time I had experienced what later I learned was called the grieving of the Holy Spirit. For me, the following days were like hell on earth. (I mean demonic hell when I say that) I felt extremely discouraged, confused, hopeless, and lost. And I had no answers for what was going on. I thought I was pleasing God by submitting to my husband. We had been doing so well until that point. What was going on?

After about three days had passed by, I was sitting in our living room and I decided to address my Christmas cards early since I had nothing else to do. I was sitting in the recliner, and my husband was lying on the floor watching TV. Suddenly, out of nowhere, the Spirit of God walked into that living room. I had only felt the Spirit of God that strong a handful of times in my life, usually in big meetings with Benny Hinn. Next, a beautiful rose fragrance permeated the atmosphere, accompanied by a light mist that felt like rain on my skin. I was tripping, to say the least. I went from feeling as if I was living in the pits of hell to walking on the streets of glory within a nanosecond. The presence of God was so strong that I was convinced even my spiritually dead husband had to sense what I was feeling in that living room at that moment. So, I looked over at him and was waiting for him to pop his head up and ask what was going on. Yet he remained engrossed in his TV program without flinching. I knew then he was not feeling what I was currently feeling. I started praying and asking God, "What are you doing here? What are you doing here?" He stayed a few minutes, and then as suddenly as God had walked into my living room, he left.

I went to my bedroom and started praying even more about what had just happened. I kept asking God what was going on because I did not understand why he was there so strongly. I then became sleepy and decided to lie down for a nap. While asleep, I had a dream, and in this dream, I saw myself yelling at my husband. We were in a terrible fight, and I grabbed several black trash bags and threw all my belongings into those big bags. Then I called my parents to come and get me. But something that really stood out in this dream was the fact that I was cursing at my husband while I was yelling at him. I had not said a curse word in several years. So, when I woke up, I dismissed it as a dream from satan because I knew I no longer cursed. I started rebuking the enemy, but I pondered on that dream most of the day. The dream would not leave my mind.

As evening approached and it got late, these thoughts started bouncing around in my mind. Could he possibly be cheating on me? I dismissed those thoughts as well, thinking, "No Paula, not him. He is not that type of man, and you know it." Yet the thoughts kept coming to my mind. So, I decided on a strategy to test the theory of him cheating on me. I told him I was going to sleep earlier than normal, and I went to the bedroom. In those days, the only cell phones we had were huge brick-sized phones, and they were far too expensive to use unless it was a dire emergency. So, I figured if he were cheating, he would use this opportunity to call his lover on the house phone while he thought I was asleep. So, as I was lying in bed, pretending to be sleeping, I would pick up the phone every five minutes to see if he might be talking to someone. Every time I picked up the phone, I heard nothing. So, after doing it for a couple of hours, I finally said, "Okay God, I give this to you. If this man is cheating on me, you deal with him." I then rolled over and went to sleep. But suddenly, an old familiar fear came over me, a fear that I had battled when I was a young child—the fear of my parents dying. I had not felt this fear in decades and had forgotten all about it until that moment. And it was so strong that I picked up the phone to call my parents to check on them. And guess what I heard on the other end of that phone? My husband and his lover talking away. He was telling her everything he wanted to do to her, in vivid, pornographic detail. They went from that topic to discussing how he was going to divorce me and when he was going to file for the divorce. The lady was giving him tips on what to tell the lawyers and how to restrict me from leaving the state with our child. They were planning everything out, from A to Z.

I kept my mouth shut, even though I felt rage boiling on the inside of me. You see, I learned years ago from Larry cheating, if you wanted information, you needed to keep your mouth shut and just listen sometimes. So, I did exactly that, even though it was extremely hard to remain silent. When the phone call was over and they hung up, it was on! That was when my dream from earlier that day came to fulfillment. I was in a full-blown rage as I experienced another of my worst fears coming to pass. I could not believe I was facing the same situation as before, this time with the father of my child. The grooming satan had used on me years prior, detonated as another lethal weapon against my soul! I was totally devastated, hurt, and filled with toxic emotions. I started screaming, cursing, and throwing things. I remember stomping on his cowboy hat he had always been so proud of because Sammy Kershaw had signed it.

He did briefly get one of his wishes—the old Paula came back—just not in the way he had expected! I screamed from the top of my lungs and told him I would rather live under a BRIDGE than to deny MY GOD! (As he had me doing during the past few days, that felt like an eternity to me!) I meant those words too and just kept screaming them over and over at him! I would rather live under a BRIDGE than deny MY GOD!

I then took the black trash bags from the kitchen and started throwing all my belongings in them. During my meltdown, my husband seemed so nonchalant. It did not seem to faze him one bit that I was taking his child and leaving him. He was emotionless, as if nobody was home inside! He did not apologize; he did not talk things out or anything. I picked up the phone to call my parents to come and get me, and they drove right over. Even though they had been working all day on their flooded home from the recent tropical storm and were tired, they still came.

That night, our church's piano player, Bill Miller, happened to be admitted into the hospital, and doctors did not think he would make it. My parents knew him, so even amid all the turmoil, I asked if we could please stop by the hospital and pray for him before going home. I have no clue why I would even do that, but I did. I was in such a state of rage, yet my heart was concerned for this man of God. So, we quickly ran into pray for him and then left to go to their house. My daughter and I made a pallet on the wooden floor. The entire house had been gutted from the mid-section down and stunk like mildew. All the furniture and beds were gone, and I felt as if we were outside camping. You could see through every single room of the house and there was no privacy at all. I looked at my surroundings and cried out, asking, "God, what did I do to deserve this? I go from a beautiful, comfortable, peaceful home to sleeping on flooded and moldy floors? What did I do? Please tell me." I felt so lost at that moment! I did not understand why God would allow these types of attacks when I had been doing so well.

The following day, I went to my daughter's elementary school with my brother-in-law. I was so thankful to God for the support my sister and her husband provided during this time. Because I was unemployed and had no money to support my daughter, I approached the receptionist's desk to ask for a free lunch application. I had been a housewife for years, and facing this financial struggle was a heavy burden. When I walked up to the desk, I saw a police officer with whom my husband and I were friends standing there. He asked me how I was doing and I just busted out crying in the middle of the hallway with a loud, nasty cry! My emotions were still so raw and all over the place. I am sure the officer thought I was crazy that day, but I did not care.

After about three to four days had passed, my daughter wanted to see her dad. So, I drove her back to the house to visit him. During those days away from him, I had been praying and asking God what he wanted me to do about the marriage. But as soon as I walked back into our house, I got mad all over again! I started cussing him out, as if it had just happened again. I told him how horrible he was as a husband and father. I hurled such hateful and poisonous words at him before I got in my vehicle to leave. The enemy and the spirit of rage had taken me over big-time! But during my fit that day, my husband seemed to have finally found a small amount of remorse. He asked me if I would please stay and talk to him. I was fuming mad and wanted nothing to do with him, let alone to stay and talk. However, I knew divorce was wrong. So, I quickly prayed a quick prayer, "God, if you want me to stay and talk to this man to see if this marriage can work, I want this vehicle to break down in this driveway right now." I meant right then, too!

Now I do not know why I prayed such a prayer as that; it was just the first thing that came to my mind. But nothing happened! The car did not stop running or break down as I prayed, so I thought I was scot-free, and I thought God had answered my prayer. But when I put the vehicle in reverse to back out of the driveway and leave, GOD is my witness, the alternator on my car froze up. I could not leave even if I wanted to. God had answered my prayer once again! And even though I did not want to work things out with Brad, I wanted to please God. I considered God my everything in life and wanted to be totally sold out to him.

Whatever God wanted, no matter how bad it hurt me, is what I ultimately wanted to do as well. My husband knew I had not eaten since I had left the house and suggested we go to one of our favorite restaurants called the Potato Patch, where they throw dinner rolls at the customers dining. So, we went and sat talking about possibly working things out as we waited for the food to come. My nerves were still extremely shot due to all that had occurred over the past few days. I was still breaking down crying at the drop of a hat and physically weak and very shaky.

When the server brought our food out, I bowed my head to pray. As my head was down praying, out of nowhere, someone from the other side of the restaurant threw a hard roll, aiming right at my head! The roll hit the wall and bounced off! I did not know who had done it, but it was not a soft throw by any means, and if I were to guess, I would venture to say it was a man who had thrown it. I played softball all my life, even as an adult, and knew that was not a random incident. It had barely missed my face. My husband was upset and called for the manager, but I told him to forget it, I just wanted to leave! My nerves could not handle any more stress, and I was about ready to snap! That should have been a telltale sign to me that day of how angry the enemy gets when people attempt to reconcile a marriage, and how angry he gets when the children of God pray. Also, how deliberate the spiritual warfare that was aimed particularly at my physical and spiritual head!

So, as you can see, this reconciliation process did not start off well. God immediately told me I needed to forgive him. I quickly realized that I was about to walk through another huge phase in my life! I was going to have to figure out how to let go and forgive a cheater, the very thing I had vowed so often that I would never do again! The only catch was I did not want to forgive him and honestly did not know how to. I cried, cried, and cried some more. I was so hurt and wounded. And worse yet, the lady he was having an affair with was a female officer who worked at his station. Every day I had to face the fact that he was going off to work and would see her. So, the satan was having a field day with my mind and emotions. One day I ended up calling this woman on the phone and giving her a piece of my mind. I was not behaving as a child of God at all, and I was allowing the enemy to work through me. In that conversation she told me that my husband had also been cheating on me with the gas station attendant on their beat. So, it did not just happen with just that one woman alone. And honestly, I am now not sure how many other women he cheated on me with or how often it had happened. According to him, it was only with those two women, but I had reasons to think otherwise from past situations that I began to recall and ponder on after the fact.

However, I felt my primary threat at that time was the female officer I had busted him on the phone with. I knew they worked together, and they had to see each other daily for work. I told my husband that I wanted to know anytime this woman tried to talk to him or even remotely breathe his name to someone. I was so full of insecurity and fear. I wanted to be kept fully informed of what was going on at his job at all times. So, the day after I called her to confront her, he informed me she had sent him messages on their work computer, slandering me and calling me names. I could not believe this home wrecker who was causing all my family issues was bold enough to reach out to my husband after our talk. This had me hotter than an old wet hen all over again! The old Paula, who loved to fight, was rising back up with all her toxic emotions, that I had been trying so hard to lie down!

I immediately called Pastor Ted and told him what was going on. I told him I was on my way to whip this officer and teach her a lesson. I asked him to please be on standby, though, in case I needed bail money. And just like a good pastor and friend, he calmed me down, telling me she was not worth going to jail. He said she had already caused enough damage to me and my family. He also explained that I could end up losing my child over such foolishness. Plus, who would really believe me over the officer in the first place? She could have easily said she had no choice but to pull her gun in self-defense because of this jealous woman who showed up raging and killed me. I had witnessed a lot of coverups within the department over the past years being married to an officer, and I knew how they covered for their own! So, I figured he was right, and I did not want to take any chances on her twisting the narrative! I decided to take Pastor Ted's advice and did not go that day. But I had also learned she was going through a divorce, and her husband worked for the same police department.

So, I told my husband, "One requirement for me to stay with you is that you call her husband and confess the affair to him personally." I felt it was only the right thing to do. I remember when my husband called him on the phone, the man recorded the phone conversation, I am sure for evidence. Their divorce was a very nasty one, and they pulled out all the punches in their custody battle. During this phone call, not only did the husband find out about the affair between my husband and his wife, but he was also told about all the other sexual encounters she had been having while on duty. My husband came clean with the fact that there were multiple affairs going on at the same time, involving his wife.

After the phone call, per another one of my requests for my husband to fully come clean properly, he also called the Louisiana Internal Affairs Department. He informed them what was going on and that it was happening on the clock. This struck a nerve with me, also for the mere fact that they get paid off taxpayers' hard-earned money. My husband informed them of several sexual encounters that had taken place in the patrol cars. Moreover, some of the encounters took place while civilians were battling to stay alive during the recent tropical storm that had devastated his district in Louisiana—a storm that claimed lives, vehicles, and even homes. IAD investigators from across the state line made a visit to our home and interviewed my husband and me both. They had to get written documentation from all the officers involved in this three-ring circus love affair. I was so glad the truth came to light. However, I was also concerned that it would hit the news media, especially when it leaked out that this was all happening on the taxpayers' dime. On top of that issue, we still had the issue with the other two officers. They were fighting each other in custody court, throwing major punches, as they slung mud at one another. They were both trying to find any ammunition against each other to help support their custody rights. I knew this information would add fuel to their custody battle, and he even asked if we would be willing to testify, if need be, in court.

I was afraid they would perhaps subpoena myself or my husband into court with them, and I would have to stand beside my husband pretending as if I was a supportive and loving wife. I felt that I could not do it, because at that time, I did not want to even be married to him, much less support him before a courtroom full of people. In my own way, I was trying to make the marriage work because I knew it was God's will, while deep down I had a heart full of hate toward him! I knew I could not stand beside him, putting on a fake smile, or having to take a witness stand while I was battling my own hell on earth. I was still trying to work out the process of forgiveness and knew I could not wear such a façade in public.

Then satan tormented my mind constantly during all this drama by lying to me and telling me this woman was pregnant with my husband's child. He whispered this lie in my ears daily for a couple of years. I would even have dreams about her being pregnant. Finally, one day God spoke to me and said, "Paula, if this were truly the case, do not you think the child would have been born by now and not just be a newborn, as the satan shows you in your mind?" At that very moment God delivered me from this lying spirit that had visited me daily to torment me with this lie. I was so thankful for him setting my mind free in that area because it was being played with all the time. But there were still other lies the enemy was telling me, that God would later help me to dismantle and replace with his truth. I found myself constantly sleeping, staying in my bed and crying! I did not want to get up and face reality. I did not want to be in the same house as him. I just wanted the pain to go away! This went on for a long time, and I kept falling deeper and deeper into depression. The same demon of depression I had once fought off in my earlier years had returned, and it returned with seven more wicked spirits than himself, just as the Bible talks about in Matthew 12:45.

My self-esteem was demolished after going through all this. I remember despising the way I looked. I hated looking into a mirror. The satan would tell me I was ugly, fat, and disgusting, and that was why Brad cheated on me. I often experienced a strong urge to get a razor blade and cut my face with it. I could feel the demons that lingered over me like a thick black cloud. All I wanted to do was die. I remember at Christmas time someone asking me what I wanted for Christmas. Immediately I heard a voice inside saying, "A bullet in my head." I did not speak it verbally, but that is what I heard, and at that time, was what I wanted. The only time I felt happiness is when I would sit and mentally plan out how I wanted to kill myself. I would also mentally plan out my funeral: the casket, what songs I wanted to play, and even down to what I would wear. These morbid thoughts, which I would often relish, would bring me so much contentment.

I recall sitting in my prayer room, trying to pray, but it was so hard, and the Heavens felt totally shut off from me! I would open up to God, and I kept telling him repeatedly how I hated my husband with every fiber of my being and all that was within me. I told God, "If you want love in my heart for him, you are going to have to put it there, because there is none!" Absolutely zero love for that man was in my heart! Bitterness had overtaken me. Yet all the while, God was still trying to deal with me about forgiving him. I still did not know how to let it go or how to move on. So, I began to fast over the situation. I knew I was in some dangerous territory because of all the hate I could feel harboring inside. I could feel the demonic oppression thick around me, and knew I needed help.

So, when I started fasting, I started off by doing just a one-day fast. Then I would attempt a three-day fast. Then I took a bigger step of faith and fasted for a couple of weeks. I would do this and then take a break and start all over again. Before I knew it, I had begun to live a lifestyle of fasting! Yet I was still battling this hatred and bitterness toward my husband. I still did not have the victory in this area of forgiveness. I finally broke down and fasted for an entire month! I figured surely if I fasted a month, I would get the victory then and my husband would be set free too! Yet after the thirty-day fast, I was still bound by bitterness. I still could not feel the presence of God like I had before this affair happened.

I was angry and believed it was all my husband's fault that I could no longer hear God's voice or feel his sweet presence. So, it made me despise him even more for coming between my relationships with God. I held my relationship with God ever so sacred and special in my heart. How dare he destroy that precious communion I had between my Heavenly Father and me. All this unforgiveness in my heart was exactly what the satan wanted from me. Bitterness was the toxic cocktail he fed me, and I still did not know that I had given satan his legal right to bring in more demonic attacks against me. This was the perfect storm, and it opened another portal of hell in my life. I began to go through another round of even deeper spiritual warfare. I started feeling as if I was losing my mind again. I started hearing voices saying horrible and demonic things. I had no clue where these voices were coming from or how they had gained access. They would say the most horrendous things that a normal human being could not even imagine. I would pray and try to rebuke them, but they would not leave. Instead, they grew stronger and even more vulgar! I began to see black shadows walking in my house. I would see plates, glasses, pots, and pans fly across my kitchen. I would duck as if I were dodging a bullet! Yet there was nothing there! I could feel as if someone was tearing off my fingernails and toenails one by one. (But they would still be there) I would then look down to see the images of my nails—toenails being ripped off — and I would again start feeling them rip off me. (Yet they were still there) I was having horrible thoughts that came not from a natural human but from demons that tormented me minute by minute. Every sexual, perverted thought imaginable was battling for control of my mind! It was disgusting and sick! I had thoughts of murder, suicide, rage, envy, stealing, and so much more! Any ungodly thought you could think of, I probably had it! Again, they were not normal thoughts, and many are just too dark to share. They were the most vulgar and sadistic thoughts you could ever imagine! They were extremely intrusive too! This happened night and day, around the clock. I had no breaks from these constant attacks against my mind! I was living in pure terror that made some of these American horror stories look like fairytales.

I could not go shopping because the demons would follow me and attack me in the stores. I had times when a panic attack from all these impulsive thoughts would hit me in the store. I would have to quickly grab something to hold me up to prevent me from falling to the ground. I begged for spiritual help from everyone I knew. It felt like I was on fire in a torture chamber mentally, and nobody knew how to put out the flames. My pastors had never seen or heard of such a magnitude of attacks in all their years of ministry. They tried to reach out to their pastor friends to ask them, and the friends had never heard of such attacks either. I could feel these demons touching me inappropriately in my genital region. I could literally feel them breathing down my back and on my skin at times. Yes, they would be touching me and breathing on my skin, but nobody was there! At nighttime, there was no rest for me there either. They would come to me in my dreams and torment me while I was sleeping! They would try to have sex with me while I was sleeping, and I could not defend myself! (This stuff might sound crazy to you, but stuff like this truly can happen and was happening to me.) I would have nightmare after nightmare! I would wake up in the middle of the night in cold sweats; I could not breathe, and utter fear would grip me! When I woke up for a few seconds, it felt as if I was getting dunked underwater in my sleep and I would try to come up for air, only to get dunked again, as I drifted off to sleep! I was afraid of staying awake and afraid of falling asleep. No matter whether I was awake or sleeping, I could not stop all this torment. I heard voices constantly telling me to do crazy things; I was mentally going off the deep end! I was so worn out from the torture chamber and having no control over my own mind.

Finally, God aligned me with some key individuals who helped me and brought much-needed clear direction. I went to a revival one night, and a prophet prayed for me. He explained to me that there was a witch who had put an assignment of witchcraft against my family and my marriage. He instructed me to go home, turn on Christian music, and listen to the Word of God or preaching. He said this would help ward off the demonic spirits and for me not to turn it off. Another prophet gave this same word to me a second time, whom I had never met before, shortly after the first one. I was told by this prophet that the witches had put an assignment on my husband to tempt him to cheat on me, to gain legal access to me through unforgiveness. This was my first experience with a witchcraft attack.

My pastors were always there praying for me, but they did not know exactly what kind of attack it was or how to combat it fully. So needless to say, I was so thankful for God using these prophets to bring more clarity to this insane situation. It brought me relief in knowing I was not crazy after all. I also had my childhood friend Mandy, who did not have a clue about witchcraft, but she was there to help me along with my pastors. Later, Pastor Betty Miller, my Aunt Myrtle's friend, became another key individual I met. She knew how to fight this type of spiritual warfare, and she had become a tremendous help!

During this time, I told my husband I did not want him to tell my family about anything that was going on with me because I knew they would try to lock me up in a mental hospital. I also told him if I ended up in a mental hospital, he did not necessarily have to come see me or remain my husband, but I had one request. I wanted him to play the Bible in my room twenty-four hours a day and never turn it off. I made him promise me he would at least do that one thing and that he would ensure our daughter was taken care of in life.

I knew this was a very serious and intense battle I was in. I had experienced nothing this bad before. I figured if I did not beat these demons, I would end up locked up in a mental hospital as a ward of the state. I had just thought the other demonic battles were bad! This was on a whole different level and a mental attack on major steroids! I had already been playing the Word of God and worship music in my ears around the clock at this point. I would play it everywhere I went, and even when I went to the store. I would go to sleep with it on, playing in my ears. It was never not on, from that day forward. I remember driving to church one time, and I was amazed that I had even found the way to my church, because my mind felt like putty. I could not think properly and did not know where I was at. Yet, I had been driving to that same church location for years! My mind was shot! My mind felt empty and blank. I felt like a deer in headlights a lot of times and 'foggy' would not do the description justice! The only time I was not feeling like this was when my mind was being filled with those intrusive voices. Not only could I not discern my physical whereabouts, but I also could not discern time. I did not know how long it would take for a normal time lapse to pass, such as five-minute or fifteen-minute increments. I can only describe these demonic attacks to the simultaneous torment of schizophrenia and Alzheimer's disease. My mind was gone!

After receiving the prophet's word though, I began to get up early every morning and started confessing the Word of God over my life. I really dug into God and began spiritual warfare. And this was a huge key to eventually getting me out of this mess. I spent no less than an hour a day just verbally speaking the Word of God over my mind, my marriage, and everything that concerned me. This did not include my worship time, prayer time, or reading time. This was just me simply confessing God's Word verbally every day and speaking what I wanted to see changed in my life. I would say aloud that I forgave my husband, and that I loved him! I would confess that I had the mind of Christ! I would confess that the witches' powers were broken over my entire family. I kept confessing the Word of God, no matter how terrible things around me looked. In Ezekiel 37, God gave us a story of an entire army that was nothing but dried, dead bones. (Just like my life looked like at this time) When the Prophet Ezekiel spoke to those bones as God commanded him to, the valley of dried, dead bones came together and lived again. There is power in speaking God's Word over your life. Proverbs 18:21 says, "Death and life are in the power of the tongue, and those who love it will eat its fruit." God spoke the very world into existence in Genesis 1. We just need to activate our faith and use this weapon. Even though I had not felt in my heart or experienced a change in my mind at that moment in time, I kept verbally confessing it daily! While I was implementing speaking God's Word over my life, I was still half out of my mind, but I kept pushing forward regardless. I refused to give up! I knew this was SINK or SWIM! It was the matter of LIFE or DEATH for me!

During this time, I remember this one night at church, where a church member by the name of Bill White walked up to me with a word. He said something so basic, yet so profound to me. My mind was still off, and I could not grasp the entirety of his words at the time, but my spirit man had grabbed a hold of them! He said, "Paula, do not forget who you are!" That hit my spirit deep down where nobody had been able to reach me! Some might not have thought much of those words he planted that night, but to me, they were golden treasures straight from the portals of Heaven! I began to pray and ask God who I was because at that point, my identity was lost. Before this, I had one snarly preacher who had asked if I was even saved during these attacks. I was so shocked at his question and even more shocked at his demeaning attitude as a preacher. He, too, was another preacher who was clueless about witchcraft and ignorant of how the demonic realm worked. But I did not know it at that time. He would come down, visiting from Missouri, and preach at our church for my pastors. Due to the enemy's use of this preacher to suggestively ask this question, I also began to question my entire identity. I did not quite understand all these witchcraft attacks I was going through, but I knew in my heart I loved God. So, I questioned my identity in God, which at times caused the warfare to increase because I was not walking in authority. We must know our authority to be effective in warfare. It is an absolute must! However, God graciously spoke to my inner man and reminded me that the Bible held my answer. I began finding Bible verses that spoke to my identity as his child. I stood on those words, and I spoke them daily, along with all my other confessions. I eventually built myself up spiritually in the area of my identity. I started walking in my God-given authority all over again. I would use the sword of the Spirit and continue to attack the demons that were attacking me. I lived a life filled with fasting, praying, worshipping, confessing, and reading God's Word!

Finally, after about two and a half years of these horrific battles, that witchcraft finally broke off me! I was able to forgive and love my husband again! I had pure love in my heart where once there was nothing but pure hatred! I was able to shut the door that I had left open through my unforgiveness. You see, the enemy knew I had a great calling on my life, as I mentioned at the start of this book. He had tried many ways to destroy me before I could fulfill that calling on my life, and this was just another one of those tactics. Again, I would like to reiterate what I said before about how the enemy was able to execute his attack in this area. The enemy knew he could not tempt me to sin at this stage of my life, so he used the witches to put an assignment on my husband. The devil knew if he could get my husband to cheat on me, the roots of bitterness from years prior of Larry cheating on me would spring up! The root of bitterness and the effects can be found in Hebrews 12:15. It is so vitally important to make sure we get free from any roots of bitterness to live a successful Christian lifestyle. My husband's spiritual house was not covered or protected by the blood of Jesus, so he was easy prey for the devil. After my husband took satan's bait, that was when I fell into my own sin of unforgiveness, which opened the door for the enemy to attack me mentally. You can also follow this up in the Word of God in Matthew 18:33–35. This passage talks about a man who refused to forgive someone, and he was handed over to the tormentors because he refused to forgive. All the enemy needs is a legal door to access, so he can stay and operate. I encourage everyone reading this book to shut any door that you may have left open to the enemy and repent quickly.

One of the biggest lessons I learned was: make sure to get all sin out of your life. I will say it repeatedly: Repent! Shut the door and apply the blood of Jesus over your life. If you do not, you leave an opening for the enemy. Proverbs 26:2 says, 'As the bird by wandering, as the swallow by flying, so the curse causeless shall not come.' This means a curse cannot prosper without a cause; you must give the enemy a legal cause for the attack to take root. Arm yourself. Put on the full armor of God described in Ephesians 6, daily. This is your shield. Carve out time to pray and read the Word; write out your confessions and speak them into the atmosphere. Know who you are and whose you are. You have authority in the name of Jesus to tread upon serpents and scorpions and over all the power of the enemy. You have authority given to you by God; use it. Last but not least, do not fear! The demonic attacks only grew worse when I walked in fear. They feed off the fear of Christians and use it as their fuel. Listen very clearly: witches and warlocks have absolutely **NO POWER OVER A TRUE CHILD OF GOD.**

Behold, I give unto you power to tread on serpents and scorpions, and over all the power of the enemy: and nothing shall by any means hurt you. Luke 10:19

SIGNS OF A WITCHCRAFT ATTACK

In this section, I would like to pause my story for a moment to share a bit about witchcraft. I want to help you identify a witchcraft attack, understand how they operate, know how to protect yourself—and more importantly, how to break the assignment.

Please note: this is only a brief overview of a massive topic. Witchcraft—often called brujería—has many faces, and some even boldly claim these practices as their "religion." But we must call it what it is: witchcraft. The primary types I have personally encountered here in the United States include Wicca, Voodoo, Santería, Black and White Magic, satanism, and Root Work (Hoodoo). While there are countless dark arts practiced globally, these are the most common in our local circles.

Regardless of the name or the "title" they wrap it in, every one of them is an open portal to the devil. They all seek to tap into a power that does not come from the Throne of God, and they all require the same thing to be defeated: the authority of a believer who is covered by the Blood of Jesus. You may hear some claiming they practice "white witchcraft," considering themselves "good witches" because they believe their spells do not harm people. Make no mistake: there is nothing good about witchcraft. Period. Whether it is labeled white or black, it is the same—the use of demonic powers that did not come from God.

For those who question if witchcraft is real, let me answer with a resounding: Yes! It is absolutely real! And yes, it can affect those who are not covered under the Blood of Jesus—a truth I will mention many times. This is why I do my best to educate people, especially the ministers of God, on how to revoke every legal access point the enemy may be using.

This education is vital because I have noticed that many, especially in Western circles, remain unaware of these tactics unless they have personally faced an attack or specifically sought out teachings on these practices. The enemy does not want anyone knowledgeable or equipped to fight this type of spiritual warfare—especially the ministers of God. If he can keep those in authority in the dark, he can continue to wreak havoc on their lives. Thus, the reason there is often spiritual turbulence when his works are being exposed.

I recall one pastor who tried to silence my warnings, only to return years later to report that his church had fallen under the very attack I had warned him of. He was no longer skittish after that; he too began teaching others how to stand, fight, and counterattack the enemy's schemes.

A KEY TO VICTORY: Avoidance brings defeat, but standing on God's Word and exercising our God-given authority brings victory. We cannot defeat an enemy we refuse to acknowledge, and we cannot cast out what we are too afraid to confront by the Blood of Jesus.

To help you recognize if you are facing such an influence, use the signs listed below. Understand: just because you experience a headache or an unexplainable smell does not always mean you are in a spiritual battle. We live in a physical world where these things have natural causes; you must discern the difference. However, when these symptoms strike suddenly without reason, linger unusually long, or manifest in recurring cycles—pause and pray. They are red flags signaling a spiritual assignment against you or your family.

Witchcraft attacks are often fueled by pure jealousy. Regardless of the motive, use the list below to decipher the tactics, and always take your findings before the Lord. The power is yours through prayer, fasting, worship, and walking in your authority.

ABOVE ALL ELSE: YOU MUST BE SAVED AND COVERED BY THE BLOOD OF JESUS to battle a witchcraft attack. You MUST be BORN AGAIN. Do not attempt to engage if you are not saved! Repent first. Remember: the enemy feeds off your fear. NEVER fear these witches or warlocks. The only time you fear them is if you are not covered under the Blood of Jesus.

Assaults on the Mind and Senses: This attack targets your clarity and your thinking. It manifests as a sudden mental fog or confusion, making it nearly impossible to think clearly, focus, concentrate, or grasp what is being said. Physically, this can show up as sudden migraine headaches, dizziness, or a "heaviness" that clouds your vision and balance. The enemy's goal is to disorient you so you cannot navigate your day or hear the leading of the Holy Spirit. When you feel this sudden demonic witchcraft cloud descend, recognize it not as simple fatigue, but as a tactical strike against your mind. Rise up and use your God-given authority to send it back to the pits of hell.

Lingering Sickness and Infirmity: This is a strategic hit against your health where you find yourself constantly sick with no natural explanation. You may feel—or even be accused of—acting like a hypochondriac because doctors cannot find a medical cause for your pain. But please realize that many times, a demonic spirit will not manifest on a medical test, X-ray, or CT scan. They prefer to hide in the shadows and then later come out to "play peekaboo" just to torment you.

Because everyone is different, these attacks can manifest in a variety of ways. Some may experience unexplained cuts, sudden sharp pains in the head or ears, nosebleeds, rashes, or boils. You might even wake up with marks on your body that were not there before you went to sleep. The enemy's goal is to use these various physical distractions to weaken your body, make you feel like you are going crazy, and discourage your spirit so you cannot fulfill your divine assignments.

When you encounter sudden symptoms that defy natural logic, do not just accept them. Take it to the Lord in prayer, rebuke the spirit of infirmity in the Name of Jesus, and command your body to come into alignment with the healing stripes of Christ.

Loss of Zeal: This attack targets both your spiritual and natural drive. You may find yourself with a sudden, unexplained lack of desire to do regular, everyday things—hobbies you once loved, your work, or even basic chores around the house. This is often accompanied by a spiritual drought where you lose the hunger to pray, read the Word, or go to church. You feel as if there is a "brass heaven" above you, where your words seem to bounce back instead of reaching the throne of God.

Division and Misunderstanding: This is a strategic strike against your support system. You will notice strange, sudden conflicts and "walls" rising up between you and those you love. A spirit of offense begins to twist your words, causing people to misinterpret your heart and leading to constant relational failure and a heavy feeling of rejection. The purpose of this witchcraft is to isolate you. The enemy knows that if he can pick you off away from the flock, you are easier to devour. By cutting you off from your spiritual covering and your prayer partners, he leaves you standing alone in the dark where he can intensify his lies without anyone there to speak the Truth over yo#5 Night Torment: Tossing and turning, insomnia, or nightmares. This often includes sleep paralysis—which is nothing more than a tormenting demon attacking while you are vulnerable.

A spiritual presence in the room: You may wake up in the middle of the night with the distinct, chilling knowledge that something—or someone—is in the room with you. The atmosphere feels heavy, and your spirit immediately goes on high alert. Often, this is a witch attempting to astral project into your private space to monitor or intimidate you. You must not cower in fear! You have the legal right to police your own atmosphere. You must speak out loud with authority: "I cut your silver cord in the Name of Jesus and by the Blood of the Lamb! I command every monitoring spirit and every witchcraft spirit to leave my property now, for this home is covered by the Blood!"#7 Monitoring Spirits: The repeated appearance of flies, snakes, roaches, spiders, or black birds and owls—whether in the physical or the spiritual realm.

Financial Leaks: You may be working hard and making good money, only to have it disappear instantly as if there are "holes in your pocket." This is a strategic witchcraft attack designed to keep you in a cycle of poverty and frustration. You are hit with strange, sudden expenses—the car breaks down, an appliance fails, or an unexpected bill arrives the moment you get a little ahead. You find yourself in a constant struggle, never able to gain ground or build a surplus. This is the work of a witchcraft spirit sent to steal your provision and keep you from being a blessing to others. It is a demonic assignment trying to choke out the abundance God has promised you.

Shadow Figures and Auditory Manifestations: This is a blatant attempt by the enemy to intimidate you and fill your home with a spirit of fear. You may see black shadows in the shape of people or creatures that dart quickly across the room and vanish. You may also experience auditory attacks—hearing footsteps, doors opening, dishes slamming and closing, or even the sounds of children laughing or crying when no one else is there. You may see a bed levitate or find scratch marks down a wall. These are simply demon spirits attempting to claim territory in your home. They want to act as if they have power and like they are bigger than God.

The Assignment of Sabotage: This attack is designed to stop your momentum just as you reach the finish line. You feel like you are finally moving forward and seeing the light at the end of the tunnel, only to have the carpet pulled out from under you at the last second. It is the "five steps forward and twenty steps back" syndrome. The purpose of this attack is to create a cycle of hope deferred that makes your heart sick. The enemy wants to weary you into thinking that progress is impossible so that you will eventually stop trying and settle for a life of defeat.

You must recognize this as a demonic blockade of witchcraft attacks and a spiritual wall; you must push through with a "violent" faith to shatter the barrier and lay hold of your breakthrough.

The Siege of the Soul: This is a spiritual attack where the enemy attempts to occupy the mind. Some can find themselves fighting sudden, extreme thoughts of sadness, rage, suicide, or even homicide. This onslaught often includes intrusive thoughts of perversion, unnatural lust, or sudden urges to hurt innocent people around you or animals—thoughts that are completely contrary to who you are in Christ. The enemy's specific goal here is not just to tempt you, but to make you feel like you are going crazy. By flooding the mind with these dark, foreign thoughts, he wants you to doubt your own sanity and character so you will retreat in shame. You must recognize that these are fiery darts from the pit of hell. Do not internalize them; instead, take those thoughts captive and cast them down, refusing to give them a voice in your life. The Assignment of the Thief: This is a strategic attack of "theft and removal" fueled by a witchcraft attack being sent that can target both your technology and your physical property. I can tell you from personal experience that since I have been working on this book, I have dealt with countless hours of spiritual warfare. While the enemy has worked hard to attack every part of it, he has worked even harder in these chapters where I am specifically exposing witchcraft. This is a real battle—and some people may think we are crazy for even saying it, but it's the truth. This stuff really does happen. I have watched as screens freeze, signals drop, and devices mysteriously cycle on and off. I have even faced the agony of files that were clearly saved being suddenly removed from the system—one time I spent eight grueling hours searching for a single document that was removed and then suddenly reappeared only after I refused to give up. But do not be deceived; these witchcraft attacks do not stop at your technology. They can transition into your physical environment, or personal belongings—absolutely anything from rings and pictures to important checks—suddenly go missing. The enemy uses this witchcraft to manufacture chaos and frustration, specifically designed to make you feel like you are going crazy. Through this cycle of things vanishing and reappearing, he intends to make you distrust your own mind and second-guess the solid truth you know. This often results in a cloudy perception and being unable to think clearly, as the enemy hopes the resulting confusion will force you to give up. But take heart! No matter how hard the thief works to steal your time or your peace, God always prevails.

Rebuke the witchcraft, command the return of what was removed in the Name of Jesus, and stay the course!

Demonic and Foul Odors: This is a manifestation where you begin smelling things that are not natural to your environment. You may suddenly be overwhelmed by the stench of dead fish, waste, or sulfur, even when there is no physical source of the smell. These foul odors are often a sign of a demonic presence or a witchcraft spirit that has been sent to your location. The enemy uses these unexplainable smells to distract you and to bring a sense of unease into your home. When you encounter a scent that does not belong and has no natural cause, recognize it as a spiritual intruder. Do not ignore it; instead, immediately rebuke it and command that foul spirit to leave and go back to the pits of hell from which it came. Plead the Blood of Jesus over your home and ask the Lord to send His warring angels to set up a guard in every room of your home and protect your gates.

Monitoring Spirits: This monitoring can also extend to other spirit-assigned animals. Cats and dogs may appear out of nowhere, sitting on your property and staring with intense, spiritually intrusive eyes. Toads may suddenly congregate at your doorstep or inside your home as a sign of a curse trying to attack you.

Aggressive infestations of rodents, such as rats or mice, can be used to bring a sense of filth and a sinister atmosphere into your space. Lizards may appear in impossible places inside your home, serving as silent observers for the enemy. In extreme cases, predatory animals like cougars have been reported prowling near property in areas where they are never naturally found.

Whether these manifestations emerge deep within your home or along the borders of your property, you must recognize them as monitoring spirits for the enemy. Do not be deceived by their location; if they appear in impossible places or owls relentlessly hit your window, use your authority to blind these spiritual eyes and command every monitoring assignment to be broken in the Name of Jesus.

Cursed Objects in Your Home: Your home is intended to be a sanctuary of peace and a tabernacle for the Holy Spirit, but the enemy is always looking for a way to violate that sacred space.

Often, we unknowingly extend an invitation to darkness through the physical objects we allow past our front door. You must realize that objects are not always spiritually neutral; many serve as paraphernalia and artifacts that function as open portals. These items carry evil spirits upon them, acting as "anchors" that give the enemy the legal access he needs to enter your dwelling and launch an attack against your life.

When you bring these cursed items into your home, you are literally inviting the spirits attached to them to take up residence in your private rooms. You must exercise extreme spiritual discernment, particularly when it comes to second-hand items. Objects found at thrift stores, antique shops, or estate sales often carry the spiritual residue of their previous owners. They can have demons and foul spirits attached to them from past rituals, occult practices, or sinful environments. Even a cross or a religious statue can be a carrier of evil if it was used in a pagan ceremony or owned by someone involved in witchcraft.

Be equally guarded when accepting gifts from others, no matter how innocent the person or the item may seem. In the realm of spiritual warfare, a witch or someone under a dark assignment will often use a gift as a "Trojan Horse." These items may be specifically cursed or "charged" to act as a point of contact for evil to enter your household. This is a strategic tactic used to gain a foothold in your life and disrupt your peace from the inside out. Do not bring every gift into your house without prayer. I once had a witch in my family, gift me a diamond ring.

There are sometimes family members, friends and even church members who are under cover witches and some you would least expect. I encourage you also to routinely walk through your house and pray, asking the Holy Spirit to lead you to any item that needs removal. Especially in your children's rooms. If you feel a check in your spirit, remove that item and destroy it immediately.

Protecting your gates means ensuring that no object in your home provides the enemy a legal right to stay.

Common Portals and Open Doors: Voodoo Dolls, The Evil Eye-Hamsa, Crystal Necklaces, Chakra Stones, Dream Catchers, tarot cards, Ouija Boards, Burning Sage, Salt for Ritual Protection, African Tribal Masks, Idols and Statues of False Gods, occult symbols, Pentagrams, Horoscopes, Zodiac Decor, Books on Spell-Casting, New Age Philosophies, Horror Movies, Tarot Cards, Divination Tools, Gifts from Occultists, Yoga Symbols, Mandalas, Feng Shui Items, Totem Poles, Skulls Used as Decor, Masonic Regalia, Incense for Meditation

Rituals, Dragon or Phoenix Figurines, Gargoyles, Native American Spirit Sticks, and Pagan Altars.

PRAYER AGAINST WITCHCRAFT AND OPEN DOORS:

Step 1: The Prayer of Repentance and Renunciation

Pray this prayer out loud first to strip the enemy of his legal rights and reclaim your God-given authority.

Heavenly Father, I come before You in the mighty name of Jesus Christ. I acknowledge that You are the Lord of my life and the Master of my home. Father, I repent for my ignorance and for any way I have allowed the enemy to gain a foothold in my life. I specifically repent for any sin that has granted legal access to witchcraft attacks, and I ask You to forgive me for the spirit of fear that I have allowed to operate in my life. I ask for Your cleansing fire to wash me white as snow.

Lord, I also choose this day to forgive every person who has hurt, betrayed, or offended me. I release them into Your hands and I refuse to carry the weight of bitterness or resentment. I break every legal right that the enemy has held over me through unforgiveness, and I close those doors forever by the power of Your Spirit.

I renounce my use of any item, or the presence of any object in my home, that has functioned as an open portal. I declare that the enemy no longer has any legal right to my atmosphere, my body, or my family. By the Blood of the Lamb, I am forgiven, I am cleansed, and I stand in the authority of Jesus Christ. In Jesus name I pray, Amen.

Step 2: The Physical Cleansing and Anointing

Now that you have repented and closed the legal doors, you have the authority to enforce the enemy's eviction.

Go through your home and physically remove every cursed object or portal the Holy Spirit has revealed to you. Once they are removed, take a bottle of anointing oil (or olive oil you have prayed over). Walk through your home and physically anoint every doorframe, every window, and your pillows. Go outside and anoint your vehicles and property gates. As you apply the oil, speak with authority and command every evil spirit and monitoring spirit to leave your property immediately! You are now enforcing the victory you just claimed in prayer.

Step 3: The Final Decree of Protection and Rejoicing

Once the home is cleansed and anointed, pray this final decree to seal your gates and celebrate your victory.

By the power of the Name of Jesus and the precious Blood of the Lamb, I break every witchcraft assignment and every curse sent against me. I thank You, God, that the witches have no power over me, and I send their attacks back to the pits of hell! Lord, Your Word says You would not suffer a witch to live, yet I ask in Your mercy that You would save their souls before it is too late.

I cut every spiritual cord, blind every demonic eye, and I close and seal every spiritual door and gate with the Blood of Jesus. I thank You, Father, that I do not have a spirit of fear, but of love, power, and a sound mind. I have the mind of Christ, and I and my entire family are covered by You. I thank You, God, that my sleep is sweet and I no longer have any nightmares or dream pollution.

I declare that I dwell in the secret place of the Most High and abide under the shadow of the Almighty. Lord, You are my refuge and my fortress, and I know You have delivered me from the snare of the fowler. Because I have made you my habitation, no evil shall befall me, and no plague shall come near my dwelling.

I stand on Your Word by faith and rejoice for all that you have done here today! I rejoice for setting me free and I declare that I am no longer under any assignment of witchcraft. I decree that whom the Son sets free is free indeed, and I thank you that Your promises are Yes and Amen! My home is now a sanctuary for the Holy Spirit, and no weapon formed against me shall prosper. I thank You, Lord, for my deliverance and for the authority I have in Christ to walk in total victory. I pray all this in Jesus' Holy Name, Amen and Amen.

Mandy and Me

PASTOR CAMMY

WHAT THEREFORE GOD HATH JOINED TOGETHER, LET NOT MAN PUT ASUNDER.
MARK 10:9

CHAPTER TEN

FRUITS OF SHATTERED VOWS

I ended up staying with my husband for another six years after discovering he had cheated. Immediately after getting caught in his adulterous affair, Brad gave his heart to God. I told him this marriage would absolutely not work without God as the center. He agreed and started going to church with me. He began singing, praying for the youth, and playing the bagpipes at church. My daughter would accompany him, singing "Amazing Grace" as her daddy played the bagpipes. It was so beautiful, and I had high hopes for his turnaround. Then, I gradually began to notice that Brad was not fully surrendered, and it appeared that he might have been acting instead. I was curious if he started going to church just to appease me and not from a true heart toward God. He confessed he had a porn addiction ever since he was a young boy. There were porn stashes hidden in random places in our home. According to him, they were all given to him by fellow police officers. I caught him returning to his pet sin on multiple occasions, like a dog returning to the vomit. He even stooped low enough to masturbate to a picture of my best friend. I kept trying my best to remain focused on my own walk with God and not allow all this to affect me. I kept forgiving him repeatedly.

One night I had a dream of a huge python snake with big yellow glowing eyes aligned all the way down its body, floating down a canal of dirty water. And the snake's eyes all turned to me in one accord, where I was standing on the bank saying, "I will be back for him." I knew it was a warning that satan would come back to tempt and seduce him again. How could he not when he had left the spiritual doors wide open? I was constantly catching Brad doing random things that made this so easy for the enemy to come back in and wreak more havoc in our lives. I caught him countless times looking at random women on MySpace. While at church, I observed him flirting with other women. But I never confronted him about any of it; I chose to just pray. The lust returned full-blown, just as the snake in the dream said it would. I felt as if the enormous battle the first time around had nearly killed me, and here we were again! When we had intercourse, it was not my husband I was with. Though he was there in the flesh, his heart was far from me. It felt as if I were intimate with a stranger. His eyes looked past me every time, and I knew he was thinking of someone else; it was a demon of lust that would oftentimes take him over. (Perhaps he was thinking of my friend again.) I did not have the mental strength to keep dealing with the addiction he was battling.

I would hit rock bottom in my faith each time I saw his demon of lust manifest. It felt as if someone was ripping out my heart, dancing on it and laughing with joy at my pain. I did not understand, and it was getting harder to cope each time. I found myself calling my friend, Mandy, and just sobbing on the phone. She would encourage me to keep going. She would tell me, "Paula, God is changing him; just hang on." Her pep talks were great therapy, but this routine went on for years. By the time six years had passed and I saw no change, I started telling her, "I do not think he is going to change, and I am losing hope." Finally, toward the end, I began telling her, "I know this is not going to change, and I cannot go on anymore." I felt like I was screaming inside for help and relief, but nobody could hear me.

That's when I met someone on social media who intrigued me. This person provided a listening ear for a weary soldier. There was only one small issue with this person: it was another man. He began to tell me how beautiful I was. He uplifted me in ways I had not been encouraged in many years! He spoke all the right words to me, and the amazing thing was—he seemed to really love God. What intrigued me most about him, though, was the fact he was a close relative of the late C.H. Spurgeon. I began to have an inappropriate online love affair with this man. It felt good in the sense that I knew my husband was finally getting paid back for his countless lustful escapades, and I was finally feeling as if I had value.

This man told me that my husband had broken our marriage vows, and biblically, I was no longer bound to him. I felt that my eyes were now enlightened, and I truly deserved better than what I had been receiving all those years from my husband. I felt like a rose that had wilted from not being watered, and someone was finally watering me with much-needed attention.

After several months of talking on the phone to this man, I began to make plans to meet him in person. I also began making plans to divorce my husband and leave the marriage. I was not leaving to be with this new man, but due to how miserable I had become in my marriage. The man was just a little icing on the devil's cake of temptation. While planning my great exodus from the marriage, I was searching for local divorce lawyers one night. I went to take a shower and forgot to close my browser—a small oversight with massive consequences. When my husband returned home from work, he noticed the open tab and asked if I planned to divorce him.

I did not expect it to go down this quickly or in this manner. I was expecting a much smoother, well-planned escape. However, I had my fill of my husband at this point and blurted out, "Yes, as a matter of fact, I am!" I told him I was sick of how he had treated me all these years and I did not deserve it anymore. I reminded him of the years I had spent being faithful, only to get paid back with utter disrespect, lies, and cheating. I confessed that I had met someone who showed me I had worth and value. I explained to Brad and made it clear that I was not leaving him to go be with the new man; I simply wanted to be free from him and the last six years of misery. I told him I was done with the heartache day after day and year after year! I had cried, begged, confessed, fasted, prayed, and believed for a change, until I could do it no longer.

This confrontation unfolded on a night when my daughter happened to be sick with another double ear infection and running a fever. In an effort to avoid a confrontation in front of her, I decided to leave the house. I did not want her to witness a fight in our home, since I always felt the home was supposed to be her safe place. I decided to drive to my sister's house late that night, planning to sleep in my vehicle since they were already in bed, and planned to return the next morning for my daughter. But when I called my parents and told them what was going on, they warned me that Brad could file on me for child abandonment for leaving her with him.

So, I returned to the house thirty minutes later. Upon arriving, I discovered she was out of her bed and had been awakened by her dad. Brad had told this poor child everything that was going on. Not only was she sick, but now she had to deal with her parents' fight. He told her that I had been cheating on him, and although she was only twelve years old, she was fully aware of what that meant. The foundation of her world was cracking. She had only known me as a mom who went to church and was faithful—a mom who ate, slept, and breathed God. Now she was being told her mom was a liar and a cheater.

I filed for divorce shortly after that night and moved in with my sister. I stopped talking to the new man pretty much immediately and never ended up meeting him in person. I had lost most of my church family and friends in the process after my husband told them what had happened. He had really painted me out to be a bad person, and yes, me talking to another man while I was married was absolutely horrible. Two wrongs never make a right, and breaking marriage vows is a serious sin. I was totally wrong for what I had done. But he failed to share with everyone the entire story of what led me into that position in the first place. He neglected to inform them about the lust addiction he struggled with from day one of the marriage. He omitted the details of his physical infidelity with multiple women. He failed to tell them how we almost lost our home when he was suspended without pay—a direct consequence of the disciplinary action from his affair. He failed to tell them how my daughter and I had to sell Christmas wreaths for food and rent money on dark, cold nights on Farm to Market 1960 in Humble alone during his suspension. He neglected to inform them about the humiliating internal affair interviews conducted by the police department. Beyond all else, he failed to tell them how I lost my mind and wanted nothing more than to die because of his infidelity. Instead, he swept those parts under the rug, so nobody knew what had really been going on all the years we were married. He knew I had not shared any of our marital struggles with anyone other than our pastors and my closest friend. On the outside, we looked like the perfect picket-fence family, when really, we were falling apart behind closed doors. Because I had kept my mouth shut all those years, it was easy for him to paint an ugly portrait of me.

Due to his tainted image, people began to turn away from me and shun me. It left me feeling completely alone with no one to rely on. I gave up on everything and started going downhill, opening the door for sin in my own life. I stopped going to church completely and started partying like I had done in high school. I backslid for a total of nine months in the bars, acting like a child of satan. Even though I found God still trying to speak to me during those times, out of His mercy. At one point, my husband appealed to the lawyers to ask me to reconsider and come back to him. I said, "Absolutely not." I did not want any part of that pain anymore. Plus, I was having fun and living it up now. I did not feel ugly and worthless anymore. I had attention from other men that I had lacked for so many years from my husband. I felt footloose and fancy-free. I remember, though, even midst of me drinking and dancing, I still found myself witnessing to the men about God. I recall one telling me as we were dancing on the dance floor, "Do you think this is a place to talk about something like that?" I replied, "I bet you would not be saying that if Jesus was to split that Eastern sky right now, now would you?" It was in my bones, even in my drunken stupidity. Meanwhile, Brad was at home, hoping I would reconsider and come back.

Then, the day came when God catapulted me out of the bars, back to where I belonged. This happened when I suddenly started seeing my husband showing up at the same bars. He would dance with other women while I was dancing with other men. Finally, I thought, "This cannot keep going like this, and I had to put a stop to it. My child is the one suffering from our ignorance, and she has suffered enough! I cannot do this to her; it is not her fault that both her parents are out here barhopping, acting like fools." So, I decided I was going to stop going to bars and be the parent that stayed home. Before this point, her dad stayed home and gave her that stability on the weekends I felt was so important for her. It did not take long, though, and he was full-blown back to his old ways. My daughter ended up catching him in the act of watching porn and saw firsthand what I had to battle all those years. After that incident, another one occurred that scared her half to death. He put his duty weapon to his head and threatened to blow his brains out as he was screaming like a maniac. She was the only one in the home at this time and only twelve years old. This was far beyond what she was used to seeing. One morning he had woken her up for school and, in a fit of rage, physically threw her up against her bedroom wall with her feet dangling. I threatened to file a police report on him if he ever touched her again like that. This threat became the very ammunition his girlfriend at the time (and later wife) would use to convince him not to have anything more to do with his daughter. If the police arrested him, they knew he would lose his job. So, she reminded him of this, and it kept my daughter at bay. I suspect the new woman detested our daughter and jealousy consumed her. She claimed it was me she had a problem with, but actions showed otherwise. She was after his undivided attention, and a daughter required his attention. At one point, she even went as far as lying by telling our daughter she was pregnant with his child. She was not pregnant at all, but knew it would hurt my daughter's feelings. In my eyes, that is just evil, intentionally trying to torment an innocent child.

Her daddy ended up moving his girlfriend in just a few weeks after he had met her. He never gave my daughter a chance to heal or adjust to this new life. They got married as soon as our divorce was final and lived right down the road from us. His new wife, however, prohibited him from attending school functions or sports events and insisted on being present whenever he was with his daughter. My daughter could not call her daddy on the phone unless he put her on speaker so the new wife could hear everything. This still goes on to this day. The new wife would accuse us of wanting money from him. Yet he had never once given any money other than his normal monthly child support. He refused to give her money for school supplies, school lunches, school clothes, or sporting events.

Despite his giving her absolutely no extra money, the wife continually accused us of seeking funds from him. He paid only child support, and that was the extent of it. I feel he would not have even paid that if he could have got away with it and kept his job!

I remember one time my daughter begging her daddy to come see her and take her to the park for her birthday. She just wanted to see him alone and spend some quality time with him. He told her no. She cried and pleaded with him for at least an hour on the phone. She kept saying, "Daddy, I just want to see you! I miss you, Daddy!" My daughter even broke down and said, "Daddy, you do not have to buy me anything for my birthday. It is not about money." (She knew the stepmom was always trying to lie to him by saying his daughter just wanted money.) So, my daughter explained to him in advance, "I just want to see you." She proceeded to tell him, "You can just get a rock and put 'Happy Birthday' on it, and that is enough for me. I just want to see you, Daddy!" But sitting before his wife so she could hear, he told our daughter, "If you cannot accept my new wife, you cannot accept me either, and I do not want to see you." Overhearing that conversation literally broke my heart for my daughter's sake!

Another time my daughter called her dad to talk to him on the phone as we were shopping. The new wife began screaming and cussing at my daughter. She was accusing my daughter of wanting her dad to buy her a new pair of shoes. My daughter had never even mentioned such a thing. In fact, my daughter knew better than to ask for money because his new wife would go into a fit of rage. The wife had just made up this lie in her own mind. I would get so angry at how heartless and evil this woman was toward my child. I would tell the new wife that my daughter deserved to have a relationship with her father, and she was trying to stop it. She informed me that her baby daddy was incarcerated, and she argued that if her own daughter could live without a father, then my daughter could as well. I cussed her out and told her how horrible a person she was.

When my daughter was in high school, a boy raped her. I was an hour away from the location where it took place. I felt my only alternative to get my daughter help quick was to call my ex-husband and ask him to go to the scene. He was closer than I was, and I had no family in the area that could get there quickly. When I arrived, he was talking to the police officer about what had happened. The officer told us we would have to take her to the hospital so they could perform a rape kit on her. My daughter asked her daddy if he could please go with us to the hospital. (I am sure his presence would have brought her great comfort.) However, Brad told her no; he was going back home. Of course, we knew it was the wife making him say no, as she always had in the past. The wife controlled him like a modern-day Jezebel on steroids.

Christmas time was the only time she really saw her dad. He seemed to step up his game during the holidays and would meet her in the driveway to do an annual gift exchange. Most of the time the gift exchange would happen weeks or months after Christmas had passed. Although it was still a kind gesture and she really appreciated it. She rarely spoke to him throughout the years.

My daughter has suffered tremendously with depression over the rejection by her father. She often repeated the same patterns as I did as a teenager, cutting herself and trying to kill herself. She had to see counselors, therapists, and psychiatrists.

As a single mother, it was extremely hard on me being alone and trying to raise this child who was so severely depressed! We had no support from him at all, except his regular monthly child support payments. I prayed constantly that one day he would help, as a father should. I truly felt that I needed his support in all that she was going through. Daily, I feared coming home and opening our front door. I never knew if I was going to walk in and find my child dead from a self-inflicted wound or not.

A few years back, when she saw her dad at another Christmas driveway gift exchange, she had multiple tattoos. His wife told my daughter how trashy her tattoos looked on her. It hurt my daughter so badly that this woman was speaking down to her, and her father was still allowing it. My daughter stated that during the rare times her father allowed her to visit, she noticed the stepmom would begin saying hateful things to her once her father left. My daughter was aware that the woman deliberately avoided saying them when her dad was nearby.

Desperate to spend an ounce of time with her daddy, my daughter did her best to ignore her. The new wife also loved to brag about how much money they had and the luxurious lifestyle they were living. She did this because she knew we struggled to make ends meet financially. My daughter and I went from living in a beautiful four-bedroom home with two thousand five hundred square feet to living in a little six hundred square foot apartment. So, she did her best to rub things in my daughter's face hoping to hurt her even more.

Things did not change with the ex-husband but continually declined. After seventeen long years with Brad, that chapter of my life was finally over. It had some amazing times and some terrible times, but they all turned out for my growth in the end scheme of things. I do not share these details in this chapter to shame Brad or his wife. I wish them nothing but the best in this life. I wish them joy from above and a personal and intimate relationship with our Lord Jesus Christ. However, I do want other single parents to realize they are not alone in these types of domestic and spiritual warfare attacks. These attacks are real, and it can feel like they will never end, but there is an expiration date to every trial we go through. My daughter and I stand as a walking testimony today to the goodness of the Lord in the land of the living. We made it through, and so can you and your children if you keep your hand in the Master's hand! You must be determined not to give up and to continue to believe in the faithfulness of your great big God! Stand on His Word in Isaiah 61:3, where God declares He will give you beauty for ashes. God loves you and God has a plan! Do not allow the enemy to cause you to throw in the towel and forfeit your treasures that abide in your treasure box!

Daughter singing Amazing Grace and daddy playing the bagipes.

For we wrestle not against flesh and blood, but against principalities, against powers, against the rulers of the darkness of this world, against spiritual wickedness in high places. Ephesians 6:12

CHAPTER ELEVEN

PREACHER AND POD BOSS

Buckle up, buttercup! After the divorce, I met a lot of interesting people, but I quickly learned that dating back in the nineties was nothing like dating today. Some of the games people played shocked me. Also, I encountered some old acquaintances and a few old flames. I reconnected with Big Tom and Shawn, whom I mentioned in previous chapters. I would like to share a couple of testimonies here about reunions many years later.

Several years after my divorce, I organized a high school reunion to be held at Los Cucos Mexican Restaurant in Kingwood. We invited graduates from the surrounding schools to take part, so we welcomed those who graduated around the same time, not just those from our class. We posted it all over Facebook and asked people to share the event. The night of the reunion, I was busy setting up the tables and was turned toward the wall when I heard an extremely deep voice say, "Hey, Paula." I had not heard this voice in over twenty years, but I

knew immediately who it was! All he had to say was, "Hey,Paula," and I knew. It was none other than Big Tom himself!

I really cared for Big Tom, and it had bothered me for all those years that I never had the chance to explain why I had broken things off so abruptly with him. I turned around, looked up, and there he was. I say "looked up" because Big Tom stood six feet seven inches tall. I could not believe he was standing in the same room with me; I was beside myself—it was like I had been star-struck! That night, Tom and I talked for hours upon hours, reminiscing in his hotel room. And no, there was nothing physical. Because I was walking with God, we spent the entire time solely filling in the gaps in our lives. I explained to him my salvation and how I became a new creation in Christ Jesus. I could finally tell him how I did not want to walk away from him when I did. I explained how my mom was so upset at us dating and made me break things off.

He shared with me all the twists and turns he had experienced since the last time we had seen each other. He had played professional football for a while, had his heart broken more times than he cared to count, and currently was on probation for drinking while driving. With a breathalyzer now installed on his beautiful, new Harley-Davidson, he paid people to blow into it on his behalf. We talked and talked all night long, as if we were two young teenagers again, back in high school. We talked until we could no longer keep our eyes open. Then, when our eyes would shut, we would quickly wake back up and pick up where we had left off. We would fall asleep again, wake back up to finish our sentences, and the cycle would repeat. He seemed to drift off way quicker than I was, though, and his eyes were staying shut longer, too. I think the poor man was just worn out—physically, mentally, and spiritually altogether.

Finally, he fell asleep for the rest of the night. For some odd reason, though, God had me praying for him that night after he had fallen asleep. God woke me up to pray; then, as soon as my eyes would shut and I would fall asleep, he would wake me back up again. I repeated the same cycle that Big Tom and I had just gone through, except this time it was with God. It felt like an all-out tug of war. I would wake up and pray for him, fall back to sleep, and then wake back up to intercede all over again. This went on until the sun came up the next morning. I questioned why the praying was so intense. I wondered if it was because God wanted to change him entirely into a new man. I did not have all the answers, but by dawn, I had surely covered him in a thick blanket of prayer. I felt so bad for him; it was as if i could feel his brokenness from life's shattered dreams. The world's brutal blows had turned his big, teddy bear heart into a dark, hollow shell.

The next morning, he informed me he had to leave out of town for work, but he wanted me to ride on his Harley-Davidson with him the following weekend when he came back to town. He had aligned his Harley-Davidson with beautiful Light-Emitting Diode lights, and I have always loved motorcycles. I was excited and told him I would—not just for the thrill of the ride, but also because I had missed him so much. I was glad to be back in his company once again. As we both pulled out of the hotel parking lot, I watched sadly as he drove off. That is when God immediately began speaking to me and instructing me: I was not to join him on the motorcycle the next weekend. He also told me to get rid of all the pictures I had taken with him and not to contact him at all.

I was so upset! I could not believe what I was hearing God instruct me to do. After all, I had waited twenty years to reconnect with this man whom I cared for so much, and now God had put the brakes on it. After arguing with the Lord for a good while, I finally told him I would obey. As instructed, I deleted all the pictures, blocked his number, and had no contact with him. I still did not understand what was going on, but God impressed on me to pray for him intensely again. That is when I realized there was some kind of danger ahead. I knew then that the all-night prayer session was me interceding over something that was about to take place in his life. I asked his sister and my close prayer warriors to please join me, as there was some sort of trouble brewing concerning him. We all bombarded Heaven on his behalf.

The next weekend, when he came back to town, another girl took my place on the back of his Harley-Davidson since I had not contacted him. They ended up in a terrible accident. They were both life-flighted to hospitals, and the girl almost died. She had to have multiple brain surgeries; I was told that if she had died; they were going to charge him with manslaughter. So yes, I ran back into Big Tom again and finally had my closure with him. I am so glad that God protected me in this situation, even when I did not understand it, at the time. I am so grateful that I chose to listen, even though my flesh was kicking and screaming for its own way.

Strangely enough, my re-encounter with Shawn also involved a motorcycle incident. I had another minister friend who met Shawn at a restaurant and came back telling me about this man she had met. Through her, Shawn and I reconnected. We hung out, and I could share with him how much it meant to me we had our relationship back in the day, even though it was very short. I shared with him that the reason it meant so much was that I had no clue how a man was supposed to really treat a woman before that time. He was always sensitive to how I felt; he listened when I spoke and did not scream at me like Larry had. After all, I was fresh out of elementary school when I went into my first long-term relationship with my abuser.

We stayed in contact after that meeting and remained friends. Then one night, God had me praying for Shawn, just as he had me praying for Big Tom. This time, I kept seeing visions of his face flashing before me like a strobe light. I knew from experience that when God would do that; it meant something critical was going on. I prayed for him for a good while and then sent him a message on Facebook asking if everything was okay. He said, "Yes. Everything is great. Why?" I said, "Because God had me praying for you just now." He said, "No, everything is fine. I am fixing to go ride my motorcycle." I left it alone, but thought it was odd.

About forty-five minutes later, my friend Johnny, who worked for the Harris County Police Department, called me. He was sitting in the parking lot of a steakhouse about thirty minutes from my place and called to ask if I wanted to join him for dinner. As we were on the phone talking, he told me, "Hey, I need to let you go. Someone just wrecked their bike right in front of me." Several minutes later, I saw a Facebook post requesting prayer for Shawn because he had just been in a motorcycle accident. I was in shock! I called Johnny back and asked him about the man who had the accident. Sure enough, it was Shawn—the very man God had me pray for moments before the wreck!

I could find firsthand information through Johnny. Despite being banged up a bit, Shawn survived without serious injuries. I know it was because Johnny was right in front of the accident, in position to assist him, along with the intercessory prayers that God had me praying. God does not always share the full details of why he wants us to pray for someone, but I have learned it is vitally important to obey.

When I could speak with Shawn shortly after his accident, I let him know Johnny was my friend. Shawn was just as shocked as I was and was so grateful for God's provision. Only God can raise a standard like that when the enemy comes in like a flood against us.

The last I heard, Big Tom and Shawn had both gone to prison. I believe they released Shawn, but Big Tom remains incarcerated. The two of them were always very kind to me and have always held special places in my heart. I still pray for them to this day and have faith that they, too, will serve the Lord.

During this time, I met some great people and some not-so-great people. However, I did meet a man named Benny who seemed to have it all together. He lived near my parents in East Texas. He told me he was a preacher and worship leader at his church but was living in a recreational vehicle due to a recent divorce. He owned his own plumbing company and seemed to be established in the area. Now, I did not picture myself living in a recreational vehicle, but I did understand that everyone goes through hard seasons in life. Heck, I had come through a few of them myself. I asked him the normal routine dating questions when we first met. How many times have you been married? How many children do you have? Do you go to church? Have you ever been arrested? Benny answered all the questions just fine and seemed to be passing everything with flying colors. I spoke to his pastors and some of his friends to verify his story. I was doing my best to get the "man-fax," so to speak. The pastor informed me that he was a good man and that he truly seemed to love the Lord.

We began dating in two thousand sixteen, and on our second date, we went to a revival service in East Texas, where my friends John and Patti Smith were preaching. He was so kind, sweet, and attentive. He did not drink, use tobacco, or swear, and those qualities were a must for me dating, and I let that be known from the start. I was looking for a sold-out man of God, and not one that just talked the talk. He was a sharp dresser and loved to spoil me—taking me out to eat and sending flowers to my job. My desk never lacked fresh flowers. And all this was so very nice, considering my financial struggles as a single mother who was barely making ends meet at the time. It was a treat for me! The ladies at work thought it was sweet too. However, when the flowers kept coming and did not stop, jealousy began to set in with my boss. She would make rude comments about my flowers among the other ladies in the office and start laughing. I just kept ignoring her because I wanted to keep my job, and after all, she was my boss.

However, I got curious how much this man was spending on these gorgeous arrangements for me. Some bouquets were breathtaking, and I knew they had to cost him a pretty penny, especially the one with the crystal cross in it. So, I looked up the flower shop's website on the internet to see the cost of the flowers. He would send them from the same florist each time. When I looked, I found out they were on average one hundred dollars a pop! When I left the office that day, my boss got on my computer to examine my search history. She saw I had been on the flower shop website and started a rumor, not just within my office but throughout the entire dealership, that I had been buying all these flowers for myself. At first, I was furious that she would do such a thing, especially as my boss and the comptroller over the dealership. Later, I learned to just laugh at the incident and pray for her root of jealousy. She was surely very deceived if she thought a single mother earning my little paycheck could afford to spend one hundred dollars each week on flowers that would soon die!

The flowers did not stop coming though; he steadily kept sending them. It was like a garden sitting on my desk week after week. Plus, he was faithful to drive three hours every weekend to meet me for church and dinner. The days he came early, he would bring Starbucks and breakfast to my job. One time when he knew I had to go to the doctor, he gave me a one-hundred-dollar bill to help me with the cost. When my car broke down, he allowed me to drive his brand-new Ford Expedition. He had such a huge heart to give. He absolutely loved feeding the homeless, which was right up my alley. I loved dating him because he seemed to love God; he was kind and generous.

He then started discussing marriage with me, but I was gun-shy on that topic. The thought of getting married was nice, but in my mind, I wanted to date for a couple of years before I got married. I had been through some crazy things in life and just wanted to really make sure I was not making a mistake. I would be dismissive anytime he brought up the topic of marriage. I then noticed he became more assertive when he spoke about the topic. It was as if he was getting aggravated for some reason. I did not know why, because we had not even been dating for a year yet. I began to notice him lying about small things. I would try not to make a big fuss over them, but it was bothering me. Despite what I was seeing, we still spoke every single day. He always started my day off with a "Good Morning, Beautiful" text and ended with "I love you and good night, My Queen." He would even send me daily pictures of the different plumbing jobs he was working on.

We did a lot of fun things together, but one thing I wanted to do with him was to take a concealed handgun license class. But he explained to me he wanted nothing to do with guns and did not believe in them. I was shocked because I owned several guns and used them to hunt with. I asked him, why not? He shared with me that his friend had died from getting shot, and he had watched him bleed out. So, I just left that topic alone. As the days went by, though, my spirit became uneasy for some reason. I was picking up in my spirit that he was hiding larger things from me, but I did not know what they were.

So, one day when he had left his iPad at the house, I picked it up and began searching for clues. I noticed a woman he had been looking up, whom I would consider being his type. She looked a lot like his ex-wife. When I asked him who she was, he immediately called me crazy. He said he had no clue who I was talking about because there was no such woman. I argued with him, told him he was lying, and told him her name. But when I went back to take a screenshot and show him the proof, I saw he had already deleted his entire history. I then knew he was indeed hiding things, as I had suspected that there were much larger issues. The red flags were becoming more frequent.

So, I told him that the following weekend I wanted us to seek counsel from my pastors. I told him I could not be in another relationship with a man who lusted and lied to me. He agreed to do just that and assured me he was not lying. All week we talked as normal. I was still fuming mad, knowing he had been lying to me, but he would send the regular good morning and good night texts, telling me he loved me, like normal. At one point, I began to think maybe I did not see it after all. Maybe I was wrong somehow.

When we first started dating, he asked if he could park his pontoon boat at my parents' house, since he did not have enough space at the recreational vehicle site. My parents agreed, since they had plenty of room on their property. So, the week prior to the meeting with my pastors, he informed my dad that someone was coming to buy the boat and they would pull the boat off his land. I thought nothing of it at all. That Thursday night we talked as normal, and he told me how much he loved me. He still acted as if he really cared for me, despite our recent arguments. I, on the other hand, was still very upset.

When Friday arrived, after texting me the same loving message he did every morning, he proceeded to tell me he was sorry, but he could not come to see me this weekend. This was not normal at all for him. He had visited me every single weekend for almost an entire year, never missing a weekend ever. I knew at that point something was wrong, and I realized that the Holy Spirit had been trying to warn me. He told me he had a customer that needed a job to be completed, and he had to stay to finish the work. I asked him to send me a picture of the job he was working on, as he normally did in times past. But as soon as I asked him, all the lights went out. He immediately blocked me from Facebook, and when I called his phone, it went straight to voicemail.

At first, I was so mad about the lies I had caught him in from days prior that I did not care. But after a few hours, I started wondering if something could be seriously wrong with him. I called someone he knew and was told he had a doctor's appointment that day and was not feeling well. So, I started worrying if he was physically ill. Then I called his son in Louisiana to ask if he had heard from his dad and told him what had happened. His son said he had not heard from his dad either and was also very worried about him. He informed me he would update me as soon as he found something out. I started to panic after talking to his son and left my job. I drove for three hours to his recreational vehicle in East Texas. When I arrived, I found his truck was gone and his RV emptied out. I was crying and so upset because I had no clue what was going on. That night I cried out to God and prayed. The hours were passing by, and I still had not heard a word! When I went to sleep that night, I had a dream of him coming back and asking me to marry him again. I believed in my heart that he would return, and my dream would come true.

A couple of days went by, and I got a message on Facebook from one of his customers who was also looking for him. He was supposed to complete their plumbing job, but he did not show up, and they had not seen him. I then began reaching out and questioning the people he knew, including his ex-wife. They informed me he had been running from the law for several months now. I was so confused when they told me this. I was like a deer in headlights again, with no clue what they were even talking about! They told me he had multiple warrants for his arrest. Come to find out, he had been stealing, taking his customers' money and not completing the jobs. One of his customers was even an elderly cancer patient, and he had even stolen from him. His actions infuriated me and his exploitation of these poor people! According to the sources, he knew the law was closing in on him. Thus, his reasoning was to rush to marry me—to give him the ability to move three hours away, hoping to avoid being captured! Now things were coming together and making sense.

Now, mind you, I had overlooked the few lies and deceptions I had caught him in before, but this was an entirely different playing field. I also found out the reason he did not want to go with me to the concealed handgun class was not because of his friend bleeding out in front of him. It was because he was an ex-felon, and by state law could not be found in possession of a firearm. The man had a mile-long rap sheet with multiple arrests, and had spent several years in the penitentiary.

And here I thought I was dating a good preacher man and worship leader. It never dawned on me to do a background check; I did not think that was necessary, especially after I had spoken to his pastors and several of his friends—another lesson learned the hard way.

Two weeks passed, and I still had no clue where he was or what in the world was going on. Then, suddenly, I was sent a picture on Facebook. In the picture, I saw my boyfriend's son and all his friends partying on the boat that someone had removed from my parents' property the day before he blocked me on Facebook, claiming someone wanted to buy it. Mind you, this is the same son who knew I had been worried sick about his dad, and the same son who said he would contact me as soon as he found out anything. The son was in on the entire scheme and knew the entire time where his dad was, because he was living with him. I guess lying ran in the family bloodline. I then scanned the rest of the picture and saw my so-called boyfriend with a beer in one hand and some woman in the other hand.

All the people partying on the boat were homosexual, except him and his new girlfriend. I felt like in the Twilight Zone. I could not believe my eyes and what I was seeing. I was so dumbfounded at the lengths they had gone to cover up, lie and pull this off. A few weeks after this, the vehicle he allowed me to drive was repossessed out of my driveway. So, I was also left without a dependable vehicle. You talk about some life disappointments again! I decided to let him go and move on.

There was another man I had talked to off and on for a few years before I met this unfaithful preacher. He had asked me out on several occasions, but I would always decline. After a few months of licking my wounds, I thought I would finally accept his offer and go on a date. We began to date and enjoyed traveling together. He owned a home healthcare agency that I helped him open, and we stayed busy. I met a lot of new people doing this, and things were good. He seemed to be another one who liked to spoil me with flowers, and he knew how to treat a woman. Yet, like others, I noticed he had a lust problem that I did not like. He ended up proposing to me with a beautiful four-carat diamond ring. I told him I would marry him ONLY if he addressed his lust issues. I bought him books to read, we prayed, and I tried to teach him how to fight the demon of lust, and we even went to church counseling together. Yet, it felt like I was in the same boat as I had been with my ex-husband. I felt as if my efforts were to no avail.

By this time a year had gone by, and I was sent another message on Facebook with the preacher man's mugshot. He had been arrested in Louisiana on Easter weekend, of all weekends! In the picture, I could see a totally different person than the one I knew. I saw anger and rage all over his face. My heart was sad because he was always so full of joy and bubbly. I had never seen such a look on his face. His countenance had truly changed. Since the crimes were committed in East Texas, they extradited him there to serve his time. I wanted nothing to do with him and had not planned on speaking to him again. Even though I still had love in my heart for him, I knew what he had done was wrong.

But one day my mother said to me, "Paula, we think perhaps he really loved you but wanted to spend all his time and money on you. That was why he took people's money and came to spend the weekends with you instead of finishing the jobs." I pondered what she said and thought about all the times he so generously spent money on me. I began to feel bad. I wondered if I had been viewing this all wrong the entire time. So, I reached out to him as a friend while in jail. The last thing I wanted to see was this man get thrown to the wolves, if he was doing this for me. I also wanted to encourage him to return to the Lord. We began to talk, and I asked him a million-and-one questions to help me understand WHY. I asked him about his long rap sheet, which he had lied about. I asked him where he had been the entire time and what he had been doing. He explained everything to me. He also told me he had always loved me and that, even while he was with the other woman, he was still checking up on me in random ways. He said he had never stopped loving me. While he was in Louisiana, he admitted that he drank and gambled constantly, but he felt that the depression that came from his previous divorce had a lot to do with his actions.

He mentioned the idea of us getting back together at some point. I told him I was dating someone at the time, but was honest and explained things were extremely rocky between us. I told him I was at the end of the road in that relationship and would soon break up with him. But I made it clear to him I would not be dating someone in jail. Furthermore, I would date no one else until I officially ended things with my current boyfriend. I did not want to commit to anything, and my focus was to encourage him in his relationship with God. However, I told him if he stayed focused on God and did things God's way, it might be a possibility after he got out. He had no clue how long he would be locked up, considering his previous felonies. I knew if he did things God's way, God could intervene and give him a light sentence. He continued to serve his time and was diligent in his devotion and prayer time, even leading a Bible study in the jail. He was given favor like Joseph had in the Bible as he was locked up. He was allowed to use the desk officer's phone to call me instead of calling collect. I remember one time I was allowed to bring an entire cheesecake from the Cheesecake Factory up to the jail for him and some of the inmates to eat. Favor like that is literally unheard of. It was evident that God was working on his behalf in many ways. In the meantime, my current boyfriend kept falling further into his lustful ways, so I finally broke up with him.

Shortly after I severed that relationship, Benny was released from jail. God had granted him favor with a short sentence, but he faced a dilemma: he had nowhere to go, and no parents or family to support him. He had a terrible childhood and learned how to survive on the streets at a young age by stealing. This is what started his extensive rap sheet of felonies. The only family that would help was his son in Louisiana. Another alternative would have been a halfway house. I really felt in my heart that if he returned to his son's, he would go right back to living in sin and doing what he was doing. I had high hopes for this man, despite all that he had done. I also knew the power of redemption through Jesus! I could not picture him in a halfway house, knowing how rough they were. He did not have a car, a job, or anything. He would have to rebuild from ground zero. Daily I could see that God's mercy was still on his life, so I opened my home up to him—though I do not recommend nor condone it at all! I thought at the time this was the only choice in an attempt to keep him on the straight and narrow path with the Lord. I told him he could sleep in the back guest bedroom until he got on his feet, and until we figured out if we wanted to pursue a relationship or not. He immediately applied for food stamps and worked as a day laborer.

Things were improving, and he did not waste any time asking me to date him again. I was still unsure about being in a relationship with him and did not want to commit to anything yet. I wanted to see some real fruit first. So, I told him perhaps if things kept improving as they were, we might be able to go to another level.

God quickly blessed him with a vehicle and a much-better-paying job. He worked extremely hard for his money. I kept seeing his daily improvements and fruit appearing on his spiritual tree. So, I agreed to date him again, but I explained to him I would not date him while he was living with me. When I told him that, he asked me to marry him, so I said, "Yes." I knew there was no way I would date him and live with him too. There are some boundaries you do not cross with God as a single Christian, and I was already pushing the envelope by opening my home to help this man. That is when we immediately went into action, planning a wedding.

Then, suddenly, I started seeing some funny activity on his end reappearing again. I found empty chewing tobacco cans appearing all over and, when confronted, he lied and said he was not dipping. This happened a few times until he knew he could no longer cover it up. He finally had to break down and admit it when he was caught red-handed with it in his mouth. He was so upset with me when I busted him. You would have thought I was the one who caused him to put the dip in his mouth. One day I asked him to return a package to Amazon for me. It was already boxed up and all he had to do was drop it off. He said he would, no problem at all. After several days, I checked the Amazon account and found the box had not been dropped off. I asked him if he had returned the Amazon box, and he said, "Yes, I did." But I knew he was lying to me. I felt led by the Holy Spirit to check his trunk. When I opened it, I found the box he claimed to have dropped off. This upset me because it was such a trivial thing to lie about, and I had already endured enough lies from him. So, I confronted him, and when I did, it was not pretty. He started yelling at me and I could not believe what was going on. I almost called the wedding off because he refused to admit the truth. I have always felt a person must fully come clean in a lie before things can be repaired properly. The wedding was only two weeks away and now I was getting cold feet! I began to pray and tell God I did not want to marry this man, if it was not his will. I asked God to please speak to me, and I begged God to direct me in the right path.

It just so happened we had church that same night, and a prophet was there we had never met before. This prophet began to prophesy over him, telling him how God was going to use him to reach the lost. Well, that made me feel a little better, but I was still skeptical about marrying him, even after that word. So, I prayed and asked God to give me a dream to confirm this. That night I had a dream of several of the church people coming to me and telling me to marry him, that he was a good man. So, I figured I had my answer. I went ahead with the wedding plans, and we got married. We both agreed that our church's annual camp meeting the following weekend would be a good choice for a honeymoon. It was a two-hour round trip just to attend the services, so this would work out great. I had also discussed with him ahead of time that I would really appreciate his help with the camp meeting duties, since I was usually the one found in the kitchen, cooking, cleaning, etc. I had been having a lot of back issues at the time and really could use the extra help. Plus, I wanted to work as a team as husband and wife, serving the church as a couple should. He agreed to help me and said it would be no problem at all. I was so excited knowing I finally had a teammate who could help and support me in ministry duties.

One thing I noticed about Benny, the preacher man, though, was he always seemed to boast and brag about himself. (Characteristics of a narcissist) Of course, I knew this came from low self-esteem, so I would just pray for him and ignore it. On this day at the camp, though, my back flared up fiercely. I was in a lot of pain and had reminded him before the service to be sure to help me when the service let out. When they dismissed service, I saw him come into the fellowship hall where I had been busy working that morning and watched him as he stood at a table talking to some of my friends. I could clearly hear him as he was bragging and boasting about himself. I politely interrupted him to ask for his assistance in the kitchen. He said he would be right there, but he never came. I waited for about thirty minutes and went over to the table a second time to ask him again. He never came the second time either. I was so upset and in so much pain by the time it was all over with; he knew I was mad. On the ride to the hotel, he asked me why I was so quiet. I told him how I was in horrible pain and how we had previously talked about my needing his help. I told him I did not appreciate him leaving me high and dry like that. He became extremely angry, and it seemed as if a switch had just flipped on him. Once we arrived at the hotel, he began to lose it. He began cursing at me and calling me all kinds of horrible names. I was in the bathroom, and he would not let me leave and was holding the door shut. He then opened the door and began throwing me around the hotel room like a rag doll and choking me. My natural reflex came out, and I hit him in his face during this fight. I screamed at him and said, "I cannot believe this is happening on our honeymoon! You have got to be kidding me!" I was devastated that this was going on when we were supposed to be making happy memories—not any more bad ones.

In the midst of this physical assault that took place, my nails were ripped off my fingers, and I had bruises left up and down my arms. I was so upset! The look on his face told me he realized what he had just done: he was fearful of me calling the police. I started screaming and telling him to leave, and he left the hotel. I did not report him because I did not want to see him go to jail again. I knew God had been working so hard on this man, and I could tell God was trying to reach him. I also knew that with his previous record of multiple felonies and recently getting out of jail, they would have thrown him in for a long time. So, I ended up calling my niece Donna, to come get me instead. We went to the nail salon to have my nails repaired before the next church service started. Even though I was not going to report him, I had decided to get the marriage annulled as soon as the camp meeting was over. I remember going to the service so hurt and crushed in my spirit at what had just transpired in that hotel room. Everyone could tell something was wrong with me, but I did not say a word. I just kept cooking, cleaning, and preparing for the next meal.

While preparing the meal in the kitchen, we were watching the service playing on the television monitor. That was when I heard another prophet, whom we had never met before, prophesying over my husband. He told him the same thing the last prophet had told him just a couple of weeks prior—how God was going to use him. I started flipping out! I thought, "No way!" I was mad at God for giving him such a great prophetic word, considering what he had just done to me in the hotel room. I asked God, "Did you not see him choking me in that hotel room? Did you pay attention to the fight we LITERALLY just had?" As if God were blind to the entire ordeal or something. That was when I started to see God's ways are much higher than my ways, and his love is far deeper than mine. God looks past a man's flesh and sees the spirit. But at that time I did not understand it, and I was mad.

When the camp meeting was over, I researched getting the marriage annulled as I had planned but found out that physical abuse was not a reason for annulment. So, I ended up staying with him and trying to make it work.

I am here to tell you that before the ink even had a chance to dry on our marriage certificate, the preacher man turned into Dr. Jekyll and Mr. Hyde because after that day, things went from bad to worse. He remained in the same bedroom he had originally started out in when he first arrived at my home. We only shared the same bedroom for a month out of the entire marriage. He would scream and curse me daily over petty things. At one point, he dragged his finger across the top of his bedroom door facing and reprimanded me like I was a five-year-old child for not dusting it for him. I could not even reach the top of his bedroom door jamb, and nobody could see it. Why would he get mad over something so little? Plus, I was working a forty-hour week at the dealership, working on my side business of graphic design, and doing ministry part time. I stayed busy constantly and was worn out. The next week I remember cooking dinner for the family, and I had asked him to please wash the big soup pot for me afterwards. It was too large for me to load with the rest of the dishes in the dishwasher. I thought that was the least he could do since I had just gotten off from work, went to the grocery store, came home to cook and loaded the dishwasher. I had done everything that night except washed that one pot that was too big for the dishwasher. He had flipped out and gave me one of the worst tongue lashings I had witnessed from him yet. He screamed and cursed at me something fierce, and it was all over asking him to wash one single pot!

I was getting cursed out what seemed to be daily at this point. I was always walking on eggshells in my own home, which was once a sanctuary where the Spirit of God dwelled. I kept thinking if I could just please him and do better, then he would stop acting the way he was acting. Yet no matter how hard I tried, nothing seemed to work. Nothing was ever good enough, and I could not make him happy. I tried so hard, to no avail. I was engulfed by the spirit of fear from the constant verbal attacks and his explosive temper. I never knew from one day to the next what I would walk into when I got off work. I did not know what I would get cursed out for next. I would work late on purpose just to avoid being around him. My body began to physically react to all the high levels of stress that I was dealing with. I could not sleep, and I started breaking out in hives that covered my entire face. I missed work on several occasions due to it. I had never in my life dealt with hives and tried to combat them with antihistamines, but they would come right back. I was not dealing with the root cause, which was the stress in the home. Not only did I start battling hives due to the stress, but I began to have panic attacks again. I would literally wake up in the morning for work and before my feet hit the floor, I would get hit with a panic attack! I would have panic attacks during the day, but especially when I was at home and he would start yelling at me. My heart would start racing, it was hard for me to breathe, and I would start shaking. See, when a spirit of fear comes into our lives through trauma, that spirit comes whenever it desires and leaves when it desires. The enemy does not care; all he cares about is trying to torment us. My doctor put me on Xanax to help calm me down during these episodes. When I took Xanax, the hives would also leave.

To top all that off, I was then diagnosed with fibromyalgia, which has been linked to high levels of stress, abuse, and post-traumatic stress disorder as well. My body felt like it was in a vice-grip and being turned. I was constantly in pain from the top of my head down to the soles of my feet. The pain was unbearable, and I knew the root was from the stress of my marriage.

Yet during this time, I was still trying my best to please him. I wanted peace in my life and to save myself from another failed marriage. I wanted to see him get healed, restored by God, and make Heaven his home. I also knew how cruel the church world could be when it came to ministers who have been divorced. They often judge them without knowing the full story behind the divorce. So, I kept pushing on and praying for God to deliver him.

One night I got up to cook something for myself in the kitchen, and he had the nerve to tell me the kitchen was closed and I could not cook at that hour of the night. Evidently, I had only set hours that I was allowed to go into the kitchen and cook. That blew me away, considering it had been my house for years before he arrived, and I was kind enough to let him move in when he had nowhere else to stay. A few times while arguing, he threatened to physically harm my family and my daughter. He told me, "That was the way the people of the streets took care of business." He said they never go directly after the person they are mad at; instead, they go after their loved ones. He directly mentioned my daughter's name while telling me this. I told him if he ever laid a finger on my child, he would find a thirty-eight slug in the back of his skull. The spirit that was operating on my husband did not like my daughter at all. He often would make derogatory comments about her and put her down. While my daughter was having to deal with this man's psychotic rages in our home, she was also battling other areas of her own personal life. The combination of these battles took a toll on her, and she tried to kill herself. She had taken the pain pills he had left in the medicine cabinet. I ran to his bedroom for help to take her to the emergency room. He woke up for a minute, informed me he was not going to be joining us, and turned right over into his bed and continued sleeping. He did not care at all that she had just tried to kill herself.

Once he asked me to watch a documentary with him about the killer clown, John Wayne Gacy. To please him, I agreed to watch it. In the documentary, they played this creepy, yet happy song while he murdered his victims. My husband would sit in the recliner and whistle that song as he stared at me, smiling ear to ear. It was as if he was deliberately trying to intimidate me and, without words, was sending a demented message. One time he told me how mad he was at his dad for doing him wrong, so he handled him prison-style. He waited until he was fully asleep, then filled up a sock full of rocks and used it to beat the man on his head. He also mentioned another occasion he wanted to kill his dad; he planned a trip back home to carry out the act, only to find out he was already dead. I knew demons were ruling this man's mind and he could cause major harm to anyone. Our home was often run as if he was the prison pod boss, or something. He often talked about his prison life, what they ate, and what went on behind bars. Once my mother was going to give me a recliner because she knew I had been wanting a new one. He told my mother and me that it would be his chair, and that my daughter and I would not be allowed to sit in it. His reasoning was that he was the king of the house, and every king should have their own chair—even though I was working just as hard as he was and the chair was going to be a gift from my mother to me. He still told my mother that it was going to be his chair. My mother gave him a piece of her mind that day, though!

My daughter got tired of the constant fighting. Her spirit was sensitive, and she could feel the tension rising in the home. She knew how dangerous his fits of rage were getting. One night when I came home from work, I thought I smelled natural gas. My husband was not home. He said he had to work late, which I found odd because he rarely worked overtime at the new company. I called my parents immediately, thinking he might have been trying to kill us with gas. My daughter did not hear our conversation because she was in a different part of the house while I was talking to them. My parents told me to grab my daughter, get outside, and call the fire department. As the firefighters arrived in their heavy gear to sweep the house for gas leaks, we stood watch on the porch. My daughter turned to me and asked, "Do you think he is trying to kill us?" When she said that, it alarmed me because that was my first thought too, and I knew she had not heard the conversation I had with her grandparents. I realized then I might need to get out of the marriage if he was not going to change. I did not want my daughter and I both to end up in a coffin. I started sleeping with a gun on my nightstand, and so did my daughter. I was on high alert now and watching everything around the house. I remembered seeing a new gas can that all of a sudden appeared. I noticed it kept moving locations, and I became scared he might be trying to burn our house down. I had a friend whose husband actually did this, and with my husband's twisted thinking, I was paying close attention to everything at that point. I also knew if my husband could beat his own dad in the head while he was sleeping and attempt to kill him, we were nothing to him. I prayed even harder for God to protect us mentally, physically, and spiritually.

My daughter and my family noticed a dramatic change in me during the two years we had been married. I had always been bold and outspoken. But after marrying him, they could tell I was fearful of him and had stopped standing up for myself.

They were right, too. I had lost who I was as a person. I even went to see a counselor to see if she could help me figure out what was wrong with him and how I could help him. I wanted him to find the freedom to live a successful Christian lifestyle and thought perhaps she could help. She said he sounded broken and needed a psychological evaluation. I truly believe he was suffering from narcissism and sociopathic tendencies, which are all rooted in the spiritual realm. I tried to convince him to go with me to visit this counselor for an evaluation, but he never did. Before this relationship, I had kept hearing people throw around the word narcissist, but I thought it was some new fad word. I honestly thought people were just hyped on this new term and making a mountain out of a molehill. Little did I know this was a real demonic battle, and I was going to learn firsthand all about it. He always put on such a good show in front of our friends, family and church. He was nice as pie with sugar rolling off his lips before others, but behind closed doors, he was a nightmare. He lived two different lives.

I felt as if I was living with satan himself in the pit of hell, and we were roommates. In addition to his double-life persona, I have failed to mention the issue we encountered with intimacy and what I felt the Lord was showing me. There were only six actual sexual encounters in the entirety of the marriage, all at the beginning and all initiated by me. I found his lack of intimacy unusual for the average man. Then, halfway into the marriage, I had a dream. In this dream, I see my husband French-kissing another man. When I woke from the dream, I was startled and began to pray. I knew I had seen the man in this dream before, but I could not remember from where. I kept praying, asking the Holy Spirit to bring it back to my memory. Then, lo-and-behold, I remembered it was a homeless man we had ministered to in Houston. He lived in one of the camps we visited and fed the homeless at. After the dream, I asked my husband to please stop visiting that particular camp. He asked me why, and I simply told him I had a dream where I felt God was warning against it. I was not going to give him the full details of the dream. To my surprise, he agreed not to visit anymore. Then, a short time later, he evidently forgot what he had agreed to. He came home and blurted out in anger that the police had made the homeless people move their campsite again. This campsite was about forty minutes from our home and not near his job, so it had to be a deliberate drive on his part. I felt the Lord was showing me my husband was bisexual. I also noticed when we visited different places that often homosexuals were drawn to him like a magnet. Random men would take great interest in him and would go above and beyond to engage with him in conversations. I had witnessed men flirting with him with me standing right in front of them. My husband would just laugh it off dismissively when I questioned this peculiar interaction. Let me say this: demon spirits know other demon spirits. They know who they can engage with and who they cannot. They were comfortable engaging with my husband, and it was evident. He had also spent many years in the penitentiary, and statistics show the longer a man is incarcerated under high security levels, the greater the probability of them engaging in a homosexual lifestyle. Of course, not all people locked up fall into this category, but I felt God was showing me that my husband did. He also had several homosexuals in his direct family bloodline, which shows a generational curse is operating behind the scenes. This is oftentimes not the fault of the individuals, but they do need to repent, break the generational curse, and be set free by God. And for goodness' sake, do not get married until you are sure of your sexual identity and discuss it with your mate. Not to mention, my husband proudly sported around his pink rose ankle tattoo, sounded gay at times when he talked, and used certain hand gestures, as those who are homosexual often do. So much so, I literally had people questioning me if my husband was gay. At the beginning, I had not really noticed all these red flags, but slowly, I began to piece the puzzle together. They always say love is blind; I must have been really blinded.

However, I felt the Lord was removing my spiritual blinders. He started guiding me on how to specifically handle the situation I was in. He wanted me to take back control over who I was as a person and for me to regain my voice. I had become a puppet on a string, just like I had been with Larry earlier in my life. In fact, God had given me a dream showing me Larry's face, and it then morphed into my husband's face. God said, "I had been dealing with the same demon that had used Larry to hurt me all those many years ago." So, I slowly started standing up for myself and speaking my mind. I was scared to stand up to him at first, but I had to "do it afraid," as Joyce Meyer likes to say. I knew standing up to him was a risk, and things would worsen before they got better. But I was prepared for his demons to manifest once he realized he could no longer control me. I knew it was part of the price I would have to pay. When I say, "stand up for myself," I am not talking about acting in an ugly manner; I mean simply being brave enough to share my thoughts or offer my opinion on a situation. I was so scared of the demon of rage on him, I would oftentimes hide in a corner, waiting for the storm to pass like a little child, and not dare open my mouth. God wanted me to get enough courage to just be me again! I knew he would either try to physically attack me, kill me, or just give up and leave before it was all over, since he had lost his power to control me. So, little by little, I started opening my mouth, and when that demon of fear would try to grip me, I would take authority over it and rebuke it in JESUS' name! I started slowly building up my confidence to speak up, even if it was at what seemed to be a snail's pace. One of the last arguments I remember having with him was when my daughter left an extremely dim nightlight on in the dining room so she could see where she was walking if she woke up at night. He woke me up at four a.m., screaming and cursing me again at the top of his lungs. He knew I did not wake up until eight a.m., and he did it on purpose, just to be vicious and mean. Normally, I would have taken the lashings from his forked tongue like I had become accustomed to doing so often, but I was changing. I got out of my bed and stood up for myself and my daughter. While he was going mad, cursing and screaming at me, I finally started giving him back what he had been dishing out to me every day. I did not swear at him, but I yelled back and show him I was not backing down anymore. From that point on, I was no longer his verbal or physical punching bag. When I stood up for myself for those few months, it drove the demons on him insane, just as I had suspected it would! I knew ahead of time I would have to endure some misery standing up for myself before it broke, but I knew where I was currently was not working, either. Please know this process was not an overnight process; it took time before I was strong enough to stand fully up against these demons and regain full freedom. I knew God had given me a battle plan, and I was determined to implement it. In the end, the battle plan prevailed. He said he wanted a divorce and was leaving me. Our marriage lasted a total of two years and was finalized on October 7, 2020. two thousand twenty. It felt like an eternity, though. This relationship taught me a lot about multiple topics. I do believe he was a good man deep in his core, but the spirits he battled from his own childhood trauma, betrayals, incarceration, and abuse still had legal access to him. I like to say, "Hurt people hurt people." He still had not fully forgiven those who had hurt him, and there were legal doors open for the enemy to operate. The demons that operated through him absolutely despised me because of the Spirit of God that dwelt in me. Again, we see here the demons trying their best to annihilate me and stop me from fulfilling my destiny. They feared the treasures I was carrying in my spiritual box to help others! The enemy did not want me carrying the gospel and winning souls for God's kingdom, nor did the enemy want my ex-husband to do the same.

I am so grateful, though, for everything I learned in this relationship and, in fact, I am grateful for what I learned in all my past relationships. Let me share a few of those things. One thing I learned is that even though it can be God's will for someone to be in ministry, married and working for the kingdom, it does not mean it is always the person's will. God can give us a roadmap and tell us where he wants us to go and what he desires for us to do, but he is not going to force the person to read that roadmap and make the right decisions. I also learned how the enemy plots in various ways. One of the plots he tried to lay out was for my daughter. He wanted to make her so miserable at home from the constant fighting and how he treated her that she would eventually move out of the home. I had explained to him from the beginning of the relationship that she lived with me and we were a package deal. The devil almost succeeded in that plot, BUT GOD!

Little did he realize, it would be him leaving, not my daughter. I learned that regardless of whether they claim to be a preacher or not, they can still be running from the law, have open warrants, and open doors for demonic activity. Many claim to be saved and believe, but even the Bible says, "You believe that there is one God; you do well. Even the demons believe—and tremble!" (James 2:19). We must do more than just believe in God. We must truly love God and keep his commandments! The Bible says: "If you love Me, keep my commandments" (John 14:15). I learned to pay close attention if you feel as if your voice is being taken from you, and act on it immediately. Do not wait until you become paralyzed and unable to speak up for yourself, bound by the demon of fear. The longer you wait to act, the longer it may take for you to be set free. If you need to get out of an abusive relationship, please seek God for guidance. You are not called to be someone's whipping post or punching bag. Reach out to your pastors or friends; do not wait until it is too late to get help. There are many other lessons that I could share with you; however, for time's sake, let me leave you with the most valuable one of all, and that is TO ALWAYS LEAN ON JESUS!

Before both divorces were finalized, my ex-husbands were already living with other women. Both men remarried less than thirty days after the divorces were final. However, I have remained single myself, up until this day. I do sincerely hope and pray they both make Heaven their homes. I have forgiven them and everyone else mentioned in this book. I thank God for the lessons they taught me. I stand on the Word of God that says, "But as for you, you meant evil against me; but God meant it for good, in order to bring about as it is this day to save many people alive" (Genesis 50:20). Through all the pain I have endured in my life, literally, it has helped me be able to save many people alive. I have been able to share my testimony and what I have learned. I have been able to encourage the hopeless. I have been able to relate to people who are lost and depressed. I have been able to pray for those who are spiritually dead and watch God resurrect their weary souls. I have seen the demon-possessed set free, and the shackles over their minds broken. These trials have truly allowed me to share the treasures within my own Treasure Box.

**Apostles:
Gene and Lorine Doyle with
Prophetess Barbara Gaines**

**At the Camp Meeting
Donna and me**

Benny and me

Long time friend Johnny and me

CHAPTER TWELVE

THE BOX OPENED

Despite every trial, I never walked alone; God was always right by my side. God has restored not only my heart, mind, and body, but has brought physical healing to both me and my family. Allow me to share these testimonies to encourage you over the next few minutes. God is not a respecter of persons, and what He has done for us, I know He will do for you.

This first testimony took place while I was still married to my first husband, Brad. Late one night, I realized my hands were not wanting to work or close properly. I had an aunt who suffered from multiple sclerosis, but I was not sure if what I was experiencing was the same thing or not. I began to worry and tried calling my pastors, but they did not answer. I also tried to call my friend Mandy, but she was asleep too. I was not sure what was going on, but I knew something major was wrong. I began to pray and ask God to wake up the prayer warriors and have them call me to pray for me.

In my mind, this was a spiritual nine-one-one moment. I sat waiting for the phone to ring with a brother or sister in Christ on the other end, yet the line remained silent. But God was not silent. The next morning when I woke up, Mandy had called and told me she had a dream of a little demon standing over me, trying to attack me last night. Her having that dream assured me that even though the prayer warriors were sleeping, God still had heard my prayer and was answering me. That gave me so much faith and peace all by itself.

I went to the doctor and was diagnosed with rheumatoid arthritis. The doctor prescribed a medication that did not help and caused all kinds of crazy side effects. I was in constant pain and prayed night after night for God to heal me. It got so bad that I could not even tie a ribbon in my daughter's hair or pick up a pitcher of tea. Then one night, the elderly man, Reverend Billy Griffin, who prophesied to me when I was a young, rebellious teenager, came back to that old family church where I was attending. He had not seen me in years and had no clue who I was. He did not realize I was the one who ran out of the church doors cussing when the power of God had hit that night so many years ago. As soon as he was done preaching, he called everyone who needed a touch from God to the front. I was the first one he called out. He prayed over me and told me God was going to heal me.

I went home, and I stood on the prophet's word, even though there were many days I did not feel healed! Many days I would be in pain, grabbing my arms and crying. Yet I would only speak and declare the Word of God over my body, no matter how badly it hurt or how I felt. I was taking my healing by faith. I knew the Bible said in Proverbs 18:21, "Death and life are in the power of the tongue, and they that love it shall eat the fruit thereof." And eventually, I was totally healed and set free from the demon of rheumatoid arthritis. This was a process of fighting the enemy off my body daily, though. It did not happen overnight, but finally, the healing manifested. Often, people who battle arthritis have given the enemy legal access to attack them through the root of bitterness and unforgiveness. I definitely was eaten up with bitterness and unforgiveness at that time in my life, thus giving the enemy open access to attack me physically. So, please be sure to pray and ask the Lord to show you if there is any unforgiveness lingering in your heart. After doing that, use the sword of the Spirit—the Word of God—to annihilate the enemy of your soul.

Another time, God removed two fibroid tumors from my uterus. One was the size of a softball, and the other, the size of a lemon. I had been going to the doctor for about seven years, trying to get relief from the pain they caused. When the doctor pumped my body full of hormones, thinking it would shrink them, it caused me to gain sixty-one pounds, yet the fibroids remained the same size. They started to become more painful and severe, disrupting my life and my job. The fibroids and endometriosis caused heavy bleeding and contributed to my anemia, which resulted in the blood transfusions I shared in the previous chapter when I had passed out.

The tumors were so painful I would have to take pain medication. I began to really pray and come against these fibroids in the spirit realm. I would speak death to the fibroids during my prayer time. I would command them to die at the root. I would thank the Lord for His Word and for healing me, even before I saw the full manifestation. One night at church, the prophet Al

Covey came to visit. He prayed over me and told me, "God is removing some things out of my body and replacing it with some new things." He said, "You are going to tell a difference." He had no clue what I had been going through, nor did he know I had a doctor's appointment the very next day.

I told my doctor that my church and I had been praying over these fibroids. I believed God had touched my body, so I requested another ultrasound to see if they were still there. His assistant told me that fibroids did not just disappear like I was thinking. I did not argue with her. I knew she was only doing her job, and I was only doing mine. I knew the proof would be in the results. When she looked at the ultrasound pictures, she was shocked! She said, "Paula, they have shrunk almost in half." None of the medications they had been pumping me full of had ever shrunk them that much. She got all excited, and you would have thought I would have too. Yet I was not. I walked out of the office and told God, "I know I should be happy about this, but I expected these tumors to be totally gone! Not just halfway gone." I told God, "I just do not understand this." I then happened to look up and saw a huge rainbow in the sky. God whispered to me in that moment to trust Him. I repented and kept speaking the Word of God over my body, but I knew God was up to something. The next time I went into the office, they found no trace of fibroids whatsoever!

God also healed me of fibromyalgia that I mentioned in the previous chapter. Studies reveal it affects women twice as often as it does men. Being that this disease flared up while I was going through my last marriage, I can attest it being linked to stress and abuse. I would pray a lot about this because it was so painful, and I did not like the medicine the doctor prescribed to treat it. This chronic disease causes painful sensations by affecting the way your brain and spinal cord process painful and non-painful signals. It causes a lot of different symptoms, but the major one is continual pain all over. My body would often go into what I considered a demonic spasm, where multiple attacks would happen simultaneously. They would start with a panic attack, followed by a fibro flare, accompanied by hives, and topped off with a debilitating migraine. It was a cocktail from hell.

The fibro flares could take days or weeks to finally calm down and stop. One time, I went to another doctor and asked him about the side effects I was experiencing from the medication for the fibro flares. Since I hated taking the medication, I tried to get off it and became extremely depressed as soon as I tried. He simply wrote down a website and instructed me to research it for myself. When I went to the website, I saw the horrific side effects. Many people on the drug were killing themselves or others. The medication was so bad that they even had support groups teaching people how to properly wean off it. I tried a few times to stop it cold turkey, but it caused my emotions to go all over the place! So, I pressed in prayer again for God to help me get off the medication and heal my body completely. After a year and a half of weaning myself off it, I was finally off the medication. And I noticed when my husband left me, the attacks were cut down by seventy percent. When they would flare up, I would speak God's Word over my body. I would come against the spirit of fear and anxiety. I would remind myself that God was in control, and everything was going to be all right. After several months of using God's Word and being free from all the stress in my marriage, I was fully set free!

Remember, the spiritual realm has effects on the physical realm. God also healed my dad of cancer. He was battling prostate cancer, and his PSA levels went up and down like a yo-yo. They removed his prostate, and we thought everything was okay. However, the cancer had spread throughout his body. I would try to encourage my daddy and tell him Jesus was going to heal him. But he would ask me, "Why would God heal me? There have been many preachers who died of cancer. God did not heal them. And how am I any different?" I told my dad I had no answers for them, but I had an answer for Him. I told him God was going to heal him. I would keep speaking this to Him. I was praying constantly for God to intervene and heal my dad. There were times I was filled with faith and just knew God was going to do it. Other times I would start sinking in my faith and start doubting, but I kept speaking the Word over Him anyhow. One night I was at the altar praying about my dad, and I could feel my faith teeter-tottering back and forth. God spoke to me and said, "Paula, your dad is not dead yet, and neither am I." I knew then that the double-minded thinking had to stop. I knew God was reaffirming that my dad was going to be healed!

My daddy seldom went to church because of the hypocrisy he had seen in the past, especially when it came to money-hungry preachers, but I begged him to go with me one night. I had never been good at directions, so I asked him to go with me to make sure I did not get lost. Well, that was one reason, but the other was because I knew there was a prophetess where we were going. I prayed that God would speak through her and perhaps God would heal my dad. I also made a vow to God that if He healed my daddy from cancer, I would never miss a church service again. My dad had just gotten back from MD Anderson Hospital that day to discuss with the doctors what kind of treatment they planned to use to fight the cancer and had taken one last test. Thankfully, he ended up going with me to church, even though it had been a long, busy day for him.

During the service, the lady prophetess, LaCricia Hvlankia, asked the congregation if anyone wanted to give a one-hundred-dollar seed, they should raise their hand. I raised my hand, and my daddy whispered to me sternly, "Paula, if you give that woman your money, I will walk out and leave you here." I was flabbergasted. He said that to me in church and shocked that he was so upset that he would leave me in downtown Houston by myself! He knew I had no clue how to get back home. She began walking down the aisle toward us while I steadily prayed for God to do something before my daddy bolted out the door. She handed me the offering envelope, and then she turned to my dad! That is when the Holy Ghost intervened and took over. She prophesied to Him for a long time; she told Him all kinds of stuff. The main thing I remembered her saying to him was that my dad would not need any treatment, and that God said He was burning it out of his body! She kept saying it over and over! God was BURNING it out of His body! I was so excited! I felt like I was on a Holy Ghost glory cloud, and victory was in the house! But when I turned to look at my daddy after she had finished and walked away, he was already walking out of the church doors! I was shocked! I did not understand! God had just spoken to Him, breakthrough was finally here, and He just walked out the door as if it never even happened!

My daddy went home and just a few days later received a phone call saying that he was cancer-free! This was nothing but a miracle from GOD! Then, after about ten years passed, the cancer tried to return. Again, I was concerned about my daddy and praying. The same lady was preaching in a tent revival off FM 2920, near Tomball, Texas. This was a lot closer, in my neck of the woods, so I went.

When she saw me, she asked if she could pray for me. Now mind you, this was many years later. I had not seen the lady in years and had never shared with her the miracle that had happened with my daddy. When she laid her hands on me, her first words were, "God said to tell you that your daddy is going to be okay." My immediate thought was, "Good grief, God had done it again, and through the same lady!" I was blown away! So afterwards, I shared the testimony with her. I explained God had healed him years prior in her meeting, but the cancer had returned. She was so excited to hear what God had done. Why on earth I did not immediately run back to that woman of God to share the testimony of His healing the first time around, I have no clue.

I later felt bad for not sharing it after seeing her rejoice the way she did. I learned then to always share with the ministers when God has done something so great in my life. Testimonies not only build the faith of the people around us but also that of the ministers. There is nothing too hard for God. These are just a few of the healings God has done for my family and me.

Prophet Al and Ronda Covey

Prophet Billy Griffin

Daddy and me

THE FINAL CHARGE

If it were possible, the enemy would love to destroy us all—physically, mentally, and spiritually. But the children of God have a hedge of protection that God has placed around us all. Psalm 34:7 says, "The angel of the Lord encamps around those who fear Him, and He delivers them." Not only do we have a hedge of protection, but we are promised that no weapon formed against us shall prosper (Isaiah 54:17).

The enemy despises God giving you treasures from Heaven and God's spiritual gifts! He despises when you carry God's anointing and you have hope, peace, joy, zeal, dreams, faith, and tenacity to share with the world. But I want to encourage you to keep walking. Know that God has not forgotten you if you have found yourself in any of these similar battles. Be reminded that everything we go through here on earth is for a season and a reason. Right now, you might not understand why the season has been so hard or even so long, but God knows.

Just like the Navy SEALs cannot allow someone to graduate to SEAL status until they have passed all their tests, they must be put under great pressure without folding or cracking. The same goes for us. God is looking for some powerful soldiers for this end-time battle. He is looking for some soldiers who are experienced in warfare! He is looking for some who has experienced pain and yet endured, so they too can help others in their hours of testing. Your pain is not in vain.

Just like we see in the book of Genesis when Joseph was betrayed by his own flesh and blood, Joseph told the very ones who hurt him, "But as for you, you meant evil against me. But God meant it for good, to bring it about as it is this day, to save many people alive" (Genesis 50:20). Joseph, in the end, was the very one who saved his family from death. So, stay encouraged and know that God is still writing your story. Know that this is not where your chapter ends. He still has good things in store for you!

We never know how God will use our stories, but we know He will. Who knows? Maybe He is going to ask you to do what He asked me to do—to share your testimony in a book for others to read, at a church service, on a radio station, at a men's or women's conference, or even to a total stranger on the side of the road. Every individual story serves as a vital weapon of offense, forged to strike back against the enemy and advance the Kingdom of God. I want to assure you that your story is a unique and powerful weapon, and the enemy fears you sharing it.

The Bible declares that the children of God overcome the devil by the blood of the Lamb and the word of their testimony (Revelation 12:11). I pray this has encouraged and enlightened you. I pray you open your heart and allow God to come in and heal any wound that might not have fully healed yet. I pray God wipes away every tear and delivers you from every fear; there is nobody who can do that for you but Jesus! He can restore you far greater than you could ever comprehend! All you need to do is trust Him and call on your Heavenly Father, who is eagerly waiting to hear from you today!

As we move forward, I invite you to join me in these targeted prayers, which are followed by some spiritual nuggets I have gathered for your journey.

INVITATION TO SALVATION:

This invitation is for everyone, no matter what you have done in your life or what you perhaps have failed to do in your life. God can forgive you! Your sin, no matter how ugly it may be, is not bigger than God. God's grace is not a reward for being perfect; it is a lifeline of love extended to those who desire to dwell with Him for all eternity. Regardless of your past or your present situation, that lifeline is a personal extension of His heart to you right now.

The Bible tells us that today is the day of salvation, and the Lord is giving you a personal invitation to secure your home in Heaven, which is waiting for you.

Perhaps you have never asked the Lord Jesus Christ into your heart before, or maybe you have, but you know your walk has grown cold and you have wandered away from Him. If that is you, please know that His arms are wide open, and He loves you. Simply join me in this prayer and mean it with all your heart.

SALVATION REDEDICATION:

Dear Heavenly Father, I know I am a sinner and in need of a Savior. I realize that I have fallen short of the glory of God and have done things my own way. I need You, and I want You to be the Lord over my life—not just for today, but for the rest of my life. I want to make Heaven my home. I ask that You come into my heart and cleanse me from all unrighteousness. I repent for all the wrong things I have done, knowingly and unknowingly.

I ask that You wash me with the redeeming and precious blood of Jesus that was shed on the cross of Calvary for my sins. I ask that You cleanse me white as snow. I believe in my heart that You raised Jesus from the dead, and I confess with my mouth today that He is my Lord. I ask that You make me a new creation in Christ Jesus, where old things have passed away and behold, all things have become new.

I ask You to guide me in every area of my life as I lay it down before You today. I choose today to serve You, and only You. I thank You that You are now the Lord over my life. I thank You for saving me and cleansing me from all unrighteousness! Thank You for writing my name in the Lamb's Great Book of Life, and thank You for loving me. I pray all this in the Holy Name of Jesus, Amen and Amen!

NEXT STEPS

Find a Church Home: If you do not have a church home, I encourage you to find one. Ask God to lead you to a Holy Spirit-filled church that believes in all nine spiritual gifts taught in 1 Corinthians 12:4–11.

Seek Experienced Leadership: You need pastors who are experienced in spiritual warfare and who know how to weather the storms the enemy throws at us. Allow them to pray for you, encourage you, and speak into your life. Jeremiah 3:15.

Be Water Baptized: I encourage you to be water baptized as a symbol of the death, burial, and resurrection of the Lord Jesus Christ. Mark 16:16

Receive the Holy Spirit: Lastly, seek the baptism in the Holy Spirit with the powerful gift of speaking in tongues, as mentioned in Acts 8:15–17.

INTERNAL HEALING PRAYER

Lord, I pray You go deep down into my heart and mind today to heal me. I pray You erase all the pain from yesterday and years that have gone by. I choose to forgive all those who have hurt me in any shape, way, or form. Lord, I know in Your Word in Matthew 6:15 it says if I do not forgive others their sins, then You will not forgive me of my sin. I truly want to go to Heaven, so I choose to forgive them today. Lord, I also know in the Bible (Luke 23:34) Jesus said, "Father, forgive them; for they know not what they do," as He was dying on the cross, and You want Your children to walk in that same level of forgiveness.

I also understand it says in Ephesians 6:12, "For we wrestle not against flesh and blood, but against principalities, against powers, against the rulers of the darkness of this world, against spiritual wickedness in high places." So, I understand the hurt that has been inflicted on me by others was the enemy using them to hurt me. I realize they were under the influence of the powers of darkness. Lord, I choose to forgive all those who have hurt me this day, and I release the hurt out of my heart into Your hands. I pray You come in and restore my mind, my will, my emotions, as well as my physical body that has been affected by this unforgiveness. I thank You Lord for delivering me from unforgiveness and any traces of bitterness. I thank You Lord for placing Your love, peace, strength, and comfort where there was once unforgiveness and bitterness. I give You praise and glory for my healing and restoration today, in Jesus' holy name, I pray, Amen and Amen!

PRAYER TO BREAK SOUL TIES

Dear God, I come before You today in the mighty name of Jesus. Lord, I thank You for the blood of Jesus that grants me all authority over the devil to destroy his works. I repent for every ungodly soul tie and relationship that I have opened the doors for and entertained. I confess my sins for allowing these unholy soul ties to be formed. I know I was wrong, and I humbly ask You to forgive me for……… (Repeat out loud what you did wrong and with whom).

In the name of Jesus, I renounce all of this and destroy every unhealthy soul tie that binds me to this person—or to anyone else, for that matter—that is not a healthy soul tie in my life. In the mighty name of Jesus, I sever every invisible chain now by the power of Jesus Christ's name and the blood of the Lamb. I set holy fire to these connections and command them to burn! I renounce every legal right I have given the enemy to attack me mentally, physically, and emotionally because of these unhealthy soul ties. I thank You, God, that I will no longer be tormented in my thoughts, dreams, or any other area in my life that is connected to these soul ties. I thank You, Lord, that I am now bound to You alone and I truly have the victory! I thank You for setting me free, and I now walk in my freedom today by faith! "Therefore, if the Son makes you free, you shall be free indeed" (John 8:36). Lord, I thank You that You have not given me a spirit of fear, but of power and of love and of a sound mind (2 Timothy 1:7). I thank You that I choose to walk in that sound mind today and forevermore. In Jesus' holy and matchless name, I pray. Amen and Amen.

PRAYER AGAINST WITCHCRAFT

Heavenly Father, I come before You in the mighty name of Jesus Christ. I acknowledge that You are the Lord of my life and the Master of my home. Father, I repent for my ignorance and for any way I have allowed the enemy to gain a foothold in my life. I specifically repent for any sin that has granted legal access to witchcraft attacks, and I ask You to forgive me for the spirit of fear that I have allowed to operate in my life. I ask for Your cleansing fire to wash me white as snow.

Lord, I also choose this day to forgive every person who has hurt, betrayed, or offended me. I release them into Your hands, and I refuse to carry the weight of bitterness or resentment. I break every legal right the enemy has held over me through unforgiveness, and I close those doors forever by the power of Your Spirit. I renounce my use of any item, or the presence of any object in my home, that has functioned as an open portal. I declare that the enemy no longer has any legal right to my atmosphere, my body, or my family. By the Blood of the Lamb, I am forgiven; I am cleansed, and I stand in the authority of Jesus Christ. In Jesus' name I pray, Amen

ENDING NUGGET ONE

Many people who suffer abuse develop what some call a Jezebel spirit. I struggled with this many years ago as well, but God set me free. This is an evil spirit that likes to control, manipulate, dominate, and seduce. It likes to rebel against those in authority and against God himself. The Bible warns us, that rebellion is as the sin of witchcraft; this can be found in 1 Samuel 15:23. So, this is a form of witchcraft all on its own. You do not have to do rituals and spells to fall into this category of witchcraft. Many are practicing witchcraft sitting on the church pews and do not even know it.

The people who have opened themselves up to this type of spirit have oftentimes been abused so badly they will vow never to allow anyone to hurt or control them again. This becomes the access point for the spirit of witchcraft and control to dominate their life. They start rebelling by handling things their own way! They try to take the place of God by protecting themselves. Someone with a Jezebel spirit will often seek revenge when a person does them wrong. I remember vowing to myself plenty of times that if a man hurt me, I would find a way to hurt him back—and ten times worse. I wanted them to pay for hurting me, and I wanted my revenge.

These individuals can also be very jealous and controlling in their romantic partnerships or friendships out of fear of losing the other person. The Jezebel spirit manifests differently in everyone; therefore, those who carry it will not always display the same characteristics. I have seen some go as far as seducing people sexually in attempts to gain what they want from their victims. Others may battle a deep desire to be seen, heard, or honored. In a work environment, you will see them acting as if they carry the title of an owner or boss, or as if they even carry a PhD when they do not. They over-inflate their self-worth. Or, if they are in the church house, they will greatly desire power, titles, spiritual gifts, and positions of authority so they can feel important. They will also be found competing against others in attempts to feel superior. They will strive for the spotlight, microphone, or podium to feed their sense of self-worth.

This is their wounds bleeding in every area of their lives. They use the spiritual things of God for all the wrong reasons. They may even put on a facade of humility while, deep down, they are full of pride. They are wearing a mask that not everyone can see through. It is a very dangerous thing to feed these types of insecurities because the demon on them will just grow stronger. It does not help that person but makes them worse. The spirit does not like to be confronted or exposed. If it feels threatened by pending exposure, it will attack the person who is exposing them vehemently through intimidation. The person who is exposing the spirit may suddenly feel fear hitting them out of nowhere and this fear is not their own. They may even begin to feel spiritually and physically weak. Or the person who has this spirit may open a full-blown slander campaign against the one who can see through them. They will tell lies about them and do their best to ruin their reputation. They will claim they are exposing them as false ministers or Christians, but it is that person carrying the spirit of Jezebel, that is the one who is false. These Jezebel spirits love to have legal access to remain active in the lives of these wounded individuals. Again, this is not the person. We do not fight against flesh and blood. The spirit wants nothing more than to forfeit the person's calling through a life filled with rebellion and destruction, continually luring them towards the pits of hell, one wound at a time.

Also, I would like to share here, a lot of practicing witches can be found in this category as well—the ones who actually practice the rituals on purpose, for their own gain. Many of them carry a divine calling to be prophets of God, and the enemy recognized that destiny long before they did. He purposefully targeted them with heartache and pain, banking on the hope that their trauma would eventually make them vulnerable to the seduction of practicing witchcraft. The enemy understands that a wounded soul often hungers for power—not to serve, but to survive, seeking a way to control their environment. They too want to ensure they are never hurt again and they want control. Witches will use their craft for protection and to get what they want out of life, but not through God's Holy power. This power only comes from satan and in the end this power will fail them. The devil will promise them largely to draw them in, but before it is all over with, he will turn on them. He does not love them and he desires to destroy them and send them to a burning hell. He never shows them the full picture.

I too was tempted by the enemy to practice witchcraft while I was in high school. I had a warlock friend who showed me his spell books, and I remember finding them so interesting. I would read them and he would teach me things. I also had fallen into the temptation of playing with a Ouija board. I was extremely fascinated by the fact that when we began to play, the planchette moved and it answered the questions we had asked it. After that day, I wanted to play and experiment with it all the time. It was drawing me like a magnetic pull, knowing there was a real supernatural power behind it. I had no clue it was demonic powers from the pits of hell. Then, out of nowhere, I had a strong urge to get rid of it and fear hit my life like a ton of bricks. After getting saved God explained that was His spirit dealing with me to get rid of it.

A witch or warlock is satan's false prophet. The enemy will always have a counterfeit for God's original. Yet again, most of the witches are called to be the real deal in God, and the enemy wanted to snag them before they tapped into their true Kingdom identity. God wants to use them and most of them are truly gifted. They have just been tricked by the enemy to use their God given gifts for the dark side.

I remember years ago I hated witches and warlocks. I was so bitter towards them due to the attack against my marriage. Yet now I know they are just wounded and hurting souls. God desires to heal them everywhere they hurt. He also desires to protect and provide for them. He desires to be their Father God love them with an unconditional love.

I am only sharing very short inserts on this page concerning witchcraft. There is so much more to say about this topic; it would require another book all on its own. But if you feel you have taken on a Jezebel spirit or if you are an actual practicing witch, please pray the prayers above and repent. God loves you and freedom can be yours right now and right where you are! All you need to do is call on the Lord Jesus Christ and mean it with your whole heart. I invite you to join me in the Prayer of Salvation and Rededication, located in the prayer section of this chapter. There is nothing you have done, that God will not forgive. I mean absolutely nothing! Make that divine exchange today and step into the rivers of God's love. Secure your home in Heaven today where you will find eternal peace.

ENDING NUGGET TWO

Abuse Is Not your Fault

Abuse is not your fault. I know some of you may have been told the abuse you have endured was your fault, and that somehow it was deserved. That is a lie; absolutely nobody deserves to be abused for any reason at all. Abuse is sometimes swept under the rug by those who should have been there to protect you, and that is unfortunate. I have witnessed victims being let down by family members, pastors, teachers, law enforcement, and society in general! To those of you who have fallen through the cracks without proper love and healing, let me say this: I am so sorry for what you had to endure. You are truly loved; your life matters, and you have worth and value in God. The King of Glory is right there beside you to heal and deliver you once and for all. Please open your heart up and allow Him to come in and do what only He can do.

FINAL DECREE

Since becoming a Christian, I have heard many testimonies that made me think, "Wow, Paula—you have not gone through anything compared to others." My story might seem as if it was a cakewalk compared to the trials that you and so many others have also endured, but trust me, it did not feel like a simple journey at the time. However, your journey is your own, and their testimonies belong to them.

Every individual story serves as a vital weapon of offense, forged to strike back against the enemy and advance the Kingdom of God.

YOUR TESTIMONY MATTERS! The enemy knows that when you lift up your voice in a shout of triumph, you will overcome him and dismantle his tactics. He shudders in pure fear, knowing that your treasures carry the power to break the chains and set the captives free; that is why he uses the spirit of fear as a tactical weapon to silence the children of God. So, please be mindful of the wiles of the devil and keep the faith! Continue to press triumphantly forward, stand boldly, and release your treasures to the world!

I pray that you soar on the wings of God's heavenly love! Remember the Bible says that you are God's chosen treasure! "But you are a chosen generation, a royal priesthood, a holy nation, His own special people, that you may proclaim the praises of Him who called you out of darkness into His marvelous light" 1 Peter 2:9.

NOW, GO AND OPEN UP YOUR TREASURE BOX AND SHARE YOUR TREASURES WITH THE WORLD!

AFTERWORD

A Letter from the Author

As you hold these final pages, I want to share a few reflections on the journey that brought us here. The lessons within this book took a lifetime to learn, but the process of bringing them to light was a whopping twelve-year journey. For the first three of those years, the call to share my testimony was like a persistent whisper—a holy unction that refused to be silenced. I simply wanted to be certain this assignment was God's divine will and that it would produce Kingdom fruit.

After three years of wrestling with that call, we visited Rock Solid Tabernacle in Willis, Texas. As I sat in the pew, quietly pondering the book once again, Pastor Gary L. Young Sr. stopped speaking and walked directly toward me. Before I could even finish my internal thought, he began to prophesy, confirming the Lord's mandate. I was stunned—God had answered me the very moment the thought crossed my mind. There was now no denying it was His will for me to write. That prophecy ignited a relentless season of spiritual warfare that manifested every time I sat down to write. However, I stand here today with a heart full of gratitude, thanking Him for sustaining me through every moment of this long and sacred birthing process. I share this triumph with you to encourage you that you, too, are capable of pulling off such a huge endeavor. Perhaps you have been hearing that still small voice calling you to write your own book. I truly pray you will yield and obey your Father. People need to hear what you have to say. God gave you a voice for a reason, and I encourage you to use it! And when you do, please don't forget to send your Sister Paula a copy. I am rooting for you!

Over the many years, I have come to realize that people are often only loaned to us for a time. Whether they were called home to Heaven or intentionally removed from my path for my own protection, I am thankful for the pivotal roles they played. I have learned to appreciate every person who crossed my bridge—the ones who loved me and even the ones who tested me—because while people may be temporary, the lessons they leave behind are eternal. This reality became even more evident during the long process of writing these pages, as several great people graduated to glory. My greatest loss was my precious mother on January 20, 2023.

Years before releasing this book, my spirit knew she would not be here to see it because her heart could not handle its contents. At times, I would consciously stagger in my writing, hesitating to finish because I knew every word written brought me one day closer to her being gone. My great Apostle and father in the Lord, Apostle Gene Doyle, who taught me the holy and reverential fear of the Lord, also passed shortly after my mother on July 23, 2023. The mighty man of valor, Prophet Al Covey, passed on September 20, 2021. While he was removed from my path, God allowed me to link arms with some of his dearest confidants—elite generals in the Lord's army who carry that same spirit of fire.

They have sharpened me and covered me in prayer. They have went to war on my behalf and my heart is full of gratitude for Ronda Covey; Pastors Joe, Barbara, and Jo Shanna Washburn; and Pastors Brooke and Beaux Jones.

I also remember Prophet Pat Galvan, who worked alongside me in the Lord's service for many years. Faithfully plowing the fields of God as a co-laborer. What a great blessing he was.

It is in this same spirit of God's faithfulness and continued restoration that, on a deeply personal note, I am seeing God slowly answer my prayers concerning my past relationships. Brad has become more involved in our daughter's life, reaching out as she prepares to welcome her first child. I continue to pray for total restoration for their relationship, believing that time is short and we must be accountable for how we love our children. As for Benny, oddly enough, he recently moved diagonally across the street from me. I have realized that when the Spirit of the Lord no longer confronts a person, the enemy ceases to be agitated. Without the friction of God's presence, those spirits no longer manifest. I look out my window and see these pieces of my history, and I am simply reminded that God's ways are not our ways.

The person I was thirty years ago is not the same person I am today, thanks be unto God. I no longer allow my emotions to trigger me as I had once done. I have learned how to surrender to the sweet Holy Spirit as He transforms me from glory to glory, as He will continue to do until He calls me home.

As you can see from my story, at one time I was an extremely broken, sinful woman who endured my fair share of trauma, bad choices, and moments where I simply wanted to give up on life. I once played spiritual Russian Roulette, with my soul, falling on several occasions. I shared these depths with you because Jesus was sent specifically to help and minister to the brokenhearted. And today, I want to be His hand and feet extended, to minister to you. The Holy Spirit empowers me to live victoriously and to be used as a vessel to share God's love, grace, and power. I want to encourage you today to never give up on God—lean on Him. My life has seen sexual abuse, demonic attacks, divorce, and so much more; yet, in every valley, I sought God and prayed for Him to show me His divine will and a way out. He proved Himself faithful and never left me through each one of those dark valleys. I want you to experience that same power of God and assurance for you. You too can have that same overcoming power. Now, please allow me to share the core truths that I have come to realize throughout the years and through God's amazing grace:

Grace is a gift that can never be earned and a mercy that never runs dry. Even though I lived a life for satan for many years and spent a lifetime running from my true calling, God's infinite mercy was there to catch me the moment I turned back. I came to realize that there was absolutely nothing I could do to deserve God's favor. I could never be good enough on my own. It is only through the precious Blood of Jesus, which washes us white as snow, that we are clothed in His righteousness. We are not defined by our mistakes, but by His sacrifice. No matter how deep you think you have fallen or how badly you feel you have messed up, God's grace is bigger than your past—and it is only a prayer away.

Nothing in this world can satisfy a soul made for God. I learned the hard way that alcohol, drugs, and temporary relationships are nothing but empty fillers. People try so many ways to numb their pain—some run to the bottle, others run to the busy-ness of life, chasing money, success, or the hollow validation of others. But these are all just masks for a deeper ache. The hollow, aching emptiness I felt inside for so many years was simply the reality of being lost and undone without Him. I was desperately trying to fill myself up with the lusts of this world, but we were not created for that—we were created to serve God. I learned that I could not find lasting fulfillment in a world that did not create me. Until I fully committed my life to Him and stopped playing games, I was only stuffing my soul with vain vanities. You can only find true peace in the One who designed you.

The Big Three Core Keys: Prayer, the Word, and the Church. I have learned that I cannot do this life without God—period. He must be the center of it all. To keep Him there, I have found three things to be non-negotiable. First, prayer is a must; it is my direct line to the heart of the Father. Second, reading my Bible is the only way to anchor my mind in Truth and keep the enemy's lies at bay. Third, finding a local church is vital; we were never meant to walk this path alone. These are the three core keys that unlock a life of victory and keep me firmly connected to the Vine. Without Him, I am nothing; with Him, I am more than a conqueror.

The battle was never truly with flesh and blood. I now understand with such clarity that people were never the true source of my pain; they were simply the instruments the enemy used to try and take me out—mentally, physically, and spiritually. When I identified the real source of the attack, I could stop fighting people and start standing against the true adversary. The most vital key to victory when I am under fire is forgiveness. The

Word of God is clear in Matthew 6:15: "But if ye forgive not men their trespasses, neither will your Father forgive your trespasses." Without forgiveness, we risk our very place in the Kingdom of God. I always tell people: there is nobody on earth worth me going to hell for. Nursing a grudge is like nursing a viper. When we refuse to forgive, it is like holding a venomous snake in our hands, hoping it reaches over to bite the person who hurt us. The reality is that the viper will strike and kill you long before it ever reaches your enemy. That unforgiveness is a poison that will destroy you from the inside out. So, forgive quickly. Remind yourself it was not the person, but the demon using the person, and walk in the freedom that only release can provide.

What the enemy meant for harm, God has used for my good. I have been forged in the fires and made new again. For years, I was like a dirty piece of black coal—something the world looked past and held in no regard—but God looked deeper and saw a diamond. He became the Master Jeweler, extracting me from the dark pits of hell where the enemy held me captive. He then allowed me to endure the crushing weight of pressure, cutting away the jagged edges of my flesh and sanding down my rough places with the power of His Holy Spirit. Finally, He breathed upon me with His anointing, applying those finishing, and polishing touches of grace. The very trials designed to destroy me became the tools God used to strengthen my spirit and refine my character. My transformation is living proof that the Lord can take the wreckage of our past and build something beautiful and strong for His Kingdom. And let me remind you: in this life, we never graduate from His teaching. So be encouraged; if God can take a life like mine and turn it into a treasure, trust me, He can do the same for you.

Surrender is the only path to true transformation. Yielding to the Holy Spirit is not a one-time event, but a daily, sometimes moment-by-moment, surrender. I will be the first to admit there were many times I did not want to yield; I was convinced my way was better, only to find that my independence was pure foolishness. Time and again, I paid a heavy price for my independence, only to realize that God's commands are not meant to restrict us—they are meant to protect us. I finally had to accept that "Daddy knows best," and the quicker I surrender to His will, the smoother the path becomes. When I speak of surrender, I am talking about every square inch of your life: what you say, what you wear, how you talk, where you go, and how you conduct yourself on the job or in your relationships. It means literally walking with the Holy Spirit and following His lead. When He instructs you to do something, do not hesitate—just do it, like the Nike commercial says. This daily yielding is what allows God to replace our frantic reactions with His stillness and our hollow self-preservation with His unshakable divine confidence. We become strengthened the moment we surrender.

Divine order is a place of divine protection. Through the process of God's transforming power, I realized that I had spent my life resisting authority—regardless of who it was, but especially when it came to men. I did this as a defense mechanism because I had been deeply hurt; I felt I had to be my own shield. Thankfully, I learned that submitting to authority is not a curse word, but a position of great spiritual power. This is exactly why the enemy works so hard to feed us lies; he tries to trick us into thinking we can "have it our way"—as if we are ordering our life experiences through a Burger King drive-through window. But God's Kingdom operates on His terms. Whether it is the authority in a marriage, a Target store manager, or the President of the United States, God's Word calls us to a spirit of alignment. We must be careful not to negate God's structure just because we have seen people misuse their power. I believe in working smarter, not harder—and stepping under His spiritual covering is the smartest move you can make.

Trust the Father by Submitting to Authority. To those who have made a vow never to submit to authority again because of past trauma—just as I did many years ago—I encourage you to pray and talk to God about the mindset you have taken on. It is not of God, and it carries heavy consequences. Give the Holy Spirit permission to come in and minister to you. While it is easy to remain a product of our past, this is a season where God is calling you out and up into a restoration of heart and mind. Crucially, God is not asking you to trust man; He is asking you to trust Him by yielding to the authority He has established. I understand the exhaustion of trying to provide your own protection, but there is a massive difference when you yield. When you allow Him to heal the broken places, you can finally step under the shield of His divine order and receive every blessing reserved for those who do things His way. But remember, the choice is yours alone. No one can open your heart for you. I pray you make that choice today; it will be one of the greatest decisions of your life. You can do this—and remember, the Holy Spirit is right there to help you.

My box is no longer a place where treasures are hidden away; it has been opened wide for the entire world to see. I did not share these depths just to tell a story, but to show you that there is no pit so deep that His arm is no longer still. If He can reach into the wreckage of my life and pull-out jewels, imagine what He is waiting to do with yours. As I close this chapter of my journey and you begin a new one in yours, remember that you are a true diamond in the Master's hand.

Have the courage to open your own box and let the world see the beauty of God's glory through you. Step out of the shadows of your past and into the brilliance of His light.

The process was long; the warfare was real. But through the Blood of the Lamb, my victory is sealed. To God be all glory, honor, and praise for all He has done and the treasures now revealed.

Paula R. Box

The Yellow Rose of Texas

She is more precious than rubies: and all the things thou canst desire are not to be compared unto her.
Proverbs 3:15

In Loving Memory of

Maxine Box

My mother was a firecracker—full of spark and spirit, carrying the soul of a warrior. From her youth, she walked in the prophetic footsteps her own mother had laid before her. Even as a teenager, the Lord marked her with a heavy calling, sending dreams to warn her of things to come. Though church hurt caused her to drift away for a season—during which she met and married my father—but the seeds God planted in her youth never died.

While she never fully stepped into the public mission God had prepared for her, I recognized the weight of the purpose she carried. I have vowed to pick up the mantle that she left behind, honoring her legacy and the generations of faithful women who went before.

My mother was a powerhouse of influence without ever standing behind a pulpit. She possessed a rare discernment and a gift of counsel; she was a vessel through whom God spoke often though. You could share the burdens of your life, and she would immediately receive wisdom from Heaven to console you, as if God was speaking through her. She was a silent blessing, rarely sharing her prophetic insights, and never with a boastful heart. I often call people like her "Undercover Brothers," but since she was my mother, she was my Undercover Mother.

The manifestations of her gift were undeniable. During a heavy storm in Nacogdoches, Texas, she felt a sudden, clear unction to move one of their vehicles out from under the double-sided carport and into the open rain.

Though she left the other vehicle where it was, she moved the first one. Moments later, a large tree limb crashed through the structure, crushing the exact spot where her car had just been.

Her prayers were equally potent. One time she petitioned Heaven for her grandson's deliverance from alcohol, just as she had for my brother years prior. In both instances, God answered through a dream. When her grandson awoke from that dream, he realized God had supernaturally broken the chains of alcohol addiction off his life. Another incident occurred on the morning of my daughter's surgery. Mama woke that morning and as she was preparing breakfast, told my father of a dream she had. She stated the doctors had found a tumor and ended the operation. Moments later, my call confirmed that exact news. She saw what was hidden before the world did.

She loved fiercely and protected her family at all costs. She proved there is no love like a mothers, and no power greater than a mother's prayer. I believe those prayers are still ringing through the clouds of Glory, being answered to this very day.

Before the ink even dried on these pages, I knew in my spirit she would not see this day. Her heart was tender, and it could not have weathered the weight of the truths I had to tell. God orchestrated the timing, ensuring this work was completed only after she was safe in His arms, shielding her from the burdens within these chapters.

She did her best to raise us according to the path she felt was right. Though I was not raised in the church, she was the catalyst God used the night she urged me to visit Houston Revival Temple. That night changed my life forever. I am eternally grateful—not just for my natural birth, but for her role as an instrument in my spiritual birth.

She was my fiercest advocate. She always loved me through the good, the bad, and the ugly. I hope to live in a way that honors the mantle you left behind, Mama. I can only imagine you smiling down, finally seeing the fruit of all your prayers.

Thank you for your sacrifices. We miss you beyond what words can describe, but we wait with joy to see you again.

"Her children arise up, and call her blessed..." — Proverbs 31:28

"And God shall wipe away all tears from their eyes; and there shall be no more death, neither sorrow, nor crying, neither shall there be any more pain: for the former things are passed away." — Revelation 21:4.

Cool Whip
Living

MEMORIES

My flowers at work

1824

GIVE
GOD
GLORY

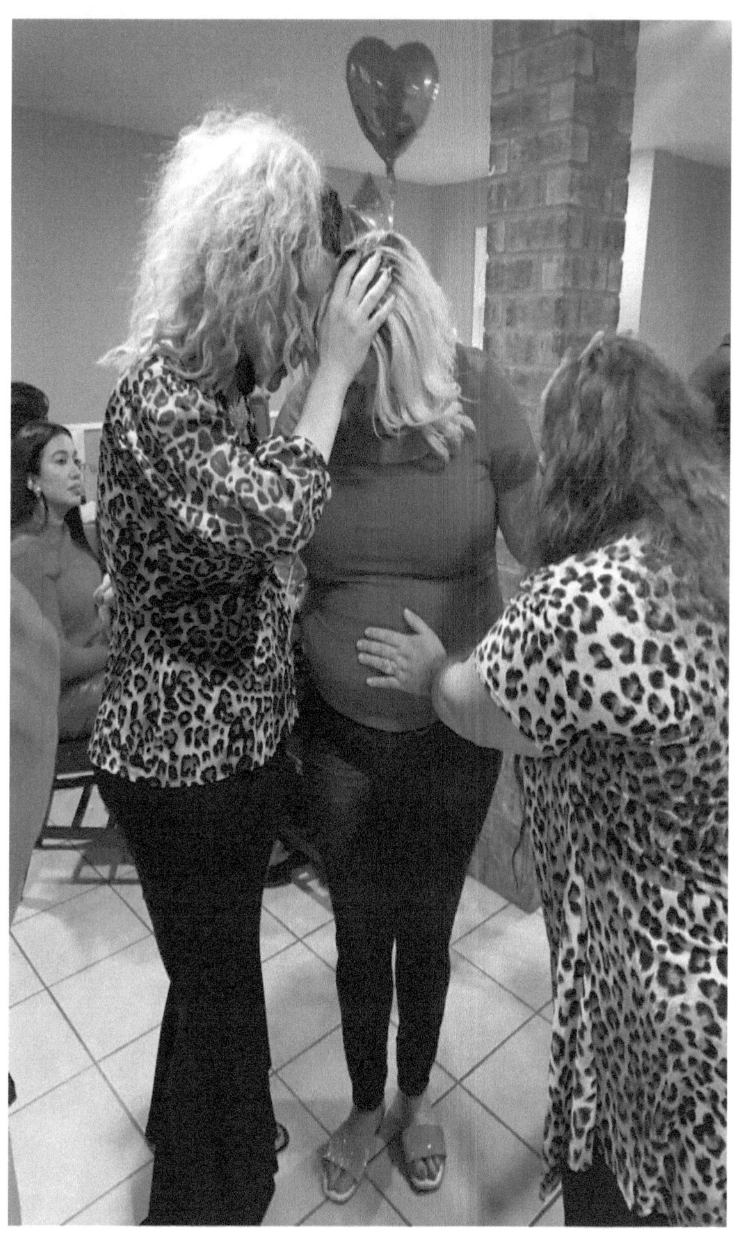

WITH
LEMON

ESUS
OVES
YOU

Pastors Joshanna Schwake - Joe and Barbara Washburn
Amity Brush Arbor Church - Belton Texas

Pastor Ted Woods, Cammy and myself.

CT A MIRACL

inspire

Togethe
We Pr

TRUST
HEART

Lakewood Church Kathy and me

Waymaker
MIRACLE WORKER
PROMISE
HER
COST
HER
COST
HER
COST

Apostles Gene and Lorine Doyle
Pastors Sam and Paula Martin
Cammy and Me

EVANGELIST PAULA R. BOX

FIREPOWER REVIVALS

But we have this treasure in earthen vessels, that the excellency of the power may be of God, and not of us.
2 Corinthians 4:7

www.ingramcontent.com/pod-product-compliance
Lightning Source LLC
LaVergne TN
LVHW090555110826
845146LV00001B/142

* 9 7 9 8 2 1 8 9 1 8 1 3 2 *